NORTHWEST
Reprints

Northwest Reprints
Series Editor: Robert J. Frank
Other titles in the series

PREFACE

but there were things
That covered what a man was, and set him apart
From others, things by which others knew him. The place
Where he lived, the horse he rode, his relatives, his wife,
His voice, complexion, beard, politics, religion or lack of it,
And so on. With time, these things fall away
Or dwindle into shadows: river sand blowing away
From some long-buried old structure of bleached boards
That appears a vague shadow through the sand-haze,
and then stands clear,
Naked, angular, itself.

from "Trial and Error," H.L. Davis

People new to a region are especially interested in what things might set them apart from others. In works by Northwest writers, we get to know about the place where we live, about each other, about our history and culture, and about our flora and fauna. And with time, some things about ourselves start to come into focus out of the shadows of our history.

To give readers an opportunity to look into the place where Northwesterners live, the Oregon State University Press is making available again many books that are out of print. The Northwest Reprints Series will reissue a range of books, both fiction and nonfiction. Books will be selected for different reasons: some for their literary merit, some for their historical significance, some for provocative concerns, and some for these and other reasons together. Foremost, however, will be the book's potential to interest a range of readers who are curious about the region's voice and complexion. The Northwest Reprints Series will make works of well-known and lesser-known writers available for all.

RJF

Dayton Hyde was the first to raise captive cranes in isolation from humans and to have such birds successfully join the wild cranes. His historic work prompted researchers working with endangered species of cranes to incorporate the use of crane-costumed humans in the isolation-rearing procedures.

These techniques are now being applied to establishing new populations of Whooping Cranes and to bolstering the numbers in remnant populations of Siberian, White-naped, and Red-crowned cranes in Asia and Wattled cranes in South Africa.

George Archibald
CO-FOUNDER, INTERNATIONAL CRANE FOUNDATION

Sandy

THE SANDHILL CRANE
WHO JOINED OUR FAMILY

by Dayton O. Hyde

with a new introduction by
Gretel Ehrlich

Oregon State University Press

Unless noted, photographs are by Dayton O. Hyde

The paper in this book meets the guidelines for permanence and durability of the Committee on Production Guidelines for Book Longevity of the Council on Library Resources and the minimum requirements of the American National Standard for Permanence of Paper for Printed Library Materials Z39.48-1984.

Library of Congress Cataloging-in-Publication Data

Hyde, Dayton O., 1925-
  Sandy : the sandhill crane who joined our family / by Dayton
O. Hyde; with a new introduction by Gretel Ehrlich.— 1st OSU
Press ed.
     p. cm. — (Northwest reprints)
  Reprint. Originally published: New York : Dial Press, 1968.
  ISBN 0-87071-486-4 (alk. paper)
  1. Sandhill crane. 2. Wildlife rescue. I. Title. II. Series.
  QL795.B57 H9 2000
  636.6—dc21
                                          00-009963

OREGON STATE
UNIVERSITY

Oregon State University Press
101 Waldo Hall
Corvallis OR 97331-6407
541-737-3166 • fax 541-737-3170
http://osu.orst.edu/dept/press

To

Gerda, Dayton, Virginia, Marsha, John, and Taylor

TABLE OF CONTENTS

For those generations yet unborn,
we are obligated to save our
endangered species from extinction.
Who among us can disclaim even
a single tiny species as being
eventually unimportant?

INTRODUCTION

Deep in the forests and meadows of the Fremont National Forest north of Klamath Falls in south-central Oregon, a young cattle rancher named Dayton O. Hyde went bird-crazy. *Sandy* is the story of how he fell in love with Sandhill Cranes and worked to save them from extinction in the 1950s when the ravages of civilization had diminished their population and put them on the endangered species list.

Grus canadensis, the Sandhill Crane is a large, long-necked marsh bird with a bald red crown, and a gray and rust body graced by a spray of wing feathers. Its long legs are the color of charcoal. Cranes wade through marshes eating young shoots and small creatures, across prairies hunting for grasshoppers, and over hummocky tundra eating insects. They mate for life and often travel in pairs. But it is their haunting, trilling cry—*garoo-a-a, garoo-a-a*—both lonely and comforting, that links us to them.

Sandy is a first-person account of that intimate engagement between human and bird. Hyde served as savior, mother hen, parent, flight instructor, and companion to the many birds who lived with him and his family at Yamsi, a wilderness ranch at the headwaters of the Upper Williamson River. No account is quite like it: Hyde observes and notates crane behavior with great fidelity and self-effacing humor. *Sandy* is a comedy of manners, a love letter to all birds and bird lovers, and a prayer for strength in the heroic measures we must all take to preserve the marshes, bogs, forests, grasslands, and rivers where these great birds thrive.

It all began one early spring evening during supper in the early 1950s at Hyde's wilderness ranch, when an old Indian cowhand mentioned a floating nest that was about to be washed away by the swelling spring river. The nest was attached to a barbed wire strung across the water and held two Sandhill Crane eggs. That night the rains came and the South Fork rose in flood. Hyde couldn't sleep and waited anxiously for dawn. He walked out across the wet meadows to the river. Reading the water, all he could see was "a sullen, white-capped torrent." Then something caught his eye. It was the Sandhill Crane hen "half submerged in the rushing sea, feathers driven askew by the current, silver gray against the clay brown of the river, eyes bewildered but determined, ready to go down with her nest."

It was then that Hyde acted as few of us would; he took off all his clothes, laid them on the snowy bank, and jumped into the frigid water. He almost drowned twice: "Clutching a passing cake of ice," he wrote, "I held for a moment, trying to rest as the current whirled my body about and swept me down towards the nest." The crane hissed at him, defending two unhatched eggs. As the nest disintegrated, Hyde grabbed the eggs. The crane lifted off and flew away, and Hyde made for shore. He hurried home with the one good egg (the other was dead) and popped it in a homemade incubator.

There began an avian love affair that continues today, inspiration for this engaging and affectionate book about the many cranes who took up residency at Yamsi, and the lush mountains and rivers of south-central Oregon where Hyde and his burgeoning family (human as well as avian) flourished.

Hyde is a man who can whistle a pigmy owl in, who can swoop up a baby porcupine into his arms without getting quills in his hands, who has nursed calves and rabbits, incubated Sandhill Crane eggs, fed children, and performed the usual ranching chores of fixing fences and tractors, harnessing a team, feeding cattle in winter, training young horses, and moving cattle from pasture to pasture with the seasons. But throughout, his eyes were always lifting to the sky, that stage whereon—to his mind—the most important enactment of the natural world took place: the coming and going of birds. Though a self-professed crane-man, he didn't care what kind of birds came. He loved them all.

Hyde was deeply influenced by the nature poetry of Alfred Noyes, whose class he took at the Cate School near Santa Barbara, and by an aristocratic aunt—Margaret Biddle—a horsewoman and naturalist who stayed with him at the family ranch. Though Hyde came into ranching through their uncle, a diehard cattleman he was not. In his own words, Hyde was "a man too easily affected by the moods of nature." He is very funny when he describes, with mock dismay, his failings as a rancher: "My eyes burn, not from watching the grazing cattle, but from staring into the skies for migrating Sandhill Cranes," he writes at the beginning of his book.

The egg he had so heriocally saved finally hatched and Sandy, the Greater Sandhill Crane for whom the book is named, came into being. Though the book is a compendium about many birds and animals, as well as the breathtaking country that comprised his wilderness ranch, it is the chapters about Sandy and his later hatchlings that are the most hilarious and affecting.

Hyde watched "breathlessly" as a small "egg tooth" poked at the shell. The bird hatched. When his wife, Gerdi, casually asked what the bird ate, Hyde drove sixty miles to the county library to look up an answer: there were no books on Sandhill Cranes in those days, and he rushed home to begin digging worms in his backyard. The crane grew and thrived. Photographs of the Hydes' first child standing with Sandy on the porch of their house and the two wading in a plastic pool show graphically how Sandy is soon the taller of the two. At maturity she was five feet tall with a wingspan of six feet.

All was well except for one thing: "She had become a crane in everything but her concept of herself—which was, of course, that she was a human," Hyde writes. Sandy had imprinted on him and the two became inseparable. He tried to teach her how to fly, flapping his elbows and running across the yard as Sandy followed. Then one day, she accidentally lifted into the air. She was free, but then again, she was in love with Hyde: she always came back.

Though cranes are described as "birds of loneliness," Sandy proved to be highly sociable. She loved outings with her human family and every year, when they went to Palo Alto for Christmas, Sandy went along, gazing at the passing scenery from the front seat. At the ranch, she supervised everything, often creating chaos when they were working cattle. Mischievious, she untied people's shoes, tore the buttons off their shirts, grabbed dogs' tails while they were sleeping.

After a few years, it was decided that Sandy ought to have a mate. A large male crane came courting and soon Red King was part of the family. There were new eggs to incubate and hatch and every one of the hatchlings imprinted on Hyde. An orphaned swan was added to the family, Whooping Cranes came and went, and at the same time, Dayton and Gerdi had more children. While the cattle operation went to hell, Hyde was "a digger of earthworms, a slicer of raw, wet liver, a referee between little roughnecks, a procurer for insatiable gourmands, a father, a mother, a psychoanalist for the emotionally unstable, and just plain slave, servant, and fall guy." A platoon of birds followed Hyde everywhere. He wrote, "We did everything in sevens."

Scenes of great hilarity continue. When Walt, a bowlegged, hard-living old buckaroo came looking for a job at Yamsi, Hyde was caught performing his daily *pas de deux* with Sandy and her young ones. Embarrassed, but undeterred, Hyde hoped that Walt would overlook this eccentricity and stay on. Despite being held prisoner in the outhouse by the birds, Walt came to accept them.

Pas de deux or *pas de sept* is perhaps the best description of this charming book. The intimacies of their comradeship are described in rich detail. Birth, childhood, love, and loss—it all happens in these pages. Some days, flapping and running with his crane-friends, Hyde seemed to be half-bird, half-man, and given the choice, would probably have opted for wings.

Throughout the book, it is clear that the curiosity went both ways. The birds could be seen flying around the second-story window of the ranch house, peering in to see what the humans were doing. They rode in the station wagon to town when Hyde went in to get supplies; they attended every human activity with vigilance and pleasure. Then one day, as winter was coming on, the young of Sandy and Red King flew away—the migratory restlessness had taken over.

For seven months, Hyde waited for them, his eyes searching the sky. Reports of cranes came in from northern California, but they were found to be herons. Finally, a sighting was reported in the newsletter of the local Audubon Society. They had been found near Bodega Bay, then taken to the Fleishaker Zoo in San Francisco. Hyde drove as fast as he could. At the zoo, he called to the birds: "Then they spotted me. Shrieking wildly, they left the other groups and flung themselves at the wire between us. A short, swarthy man in a knitted cap stared in disbelief. 'Say, mister,' he said excitedly. 'Them birds knows you.' "

Through rush hour traffic, Hyde, his car full of cranes, began his trip home. When a cop stopped him, Hyde replied coolly to his enquiries: "We're greater Sandhill Cranes and it's spring. We're migrating north." The cranes shrieked with delight in agreement, and after some confusion, they continued on. The toll gate gave them trouble, Hyde reported. Every time he handed the gate man a quarter, one of the birds tried to steal it. The toll-taker finally waved them through, but Hyde, always a man of honor, threw the quarter out of the window at the toll booth and drove north.

One might wonder at Gerdi's patience throughout, raising children while Dayton played with the birds. The book goes on to describe the rivers and forests that were part of Yamsi, the remnant culture of the first people who lived there-Native Americans-and the ways in which we must preserve wetlands and open country to accommodate what Hyde makes us see as the large, extended family of birds, animals, and humans.

Hyde reminds us of the senseless war between environmentalists and ranchers, agriculture and the public, when solutions, not conflict, are desperately needed to save both habitats and species. Both sides need to do their homework. Throughout the book, we learn the ways in which ranch life engenders both learning and patience. Ranches, when run with an understanding of whole ecosystems and an eye toward maintaining the health of the whole, not simply for the financial value of production, can serve as natural sanctuaries for wildlife. Ranches are miniature societies that can be inclusive: the Hyde family unit expanded to include lonely cowboys, summer workers, birds, horses, dogs, porcupines, deer, elk, beaver, fish, and cattle with a sense of equality that runs through all sentient beings.

Sandy was originally published in 1968 by Hyde as "the true story of the rare Sandhill Crane that joined our family." More than three decades later, the book is still a treasure: unpretentious, tenderhearted, funny, idiosyncratic, but above all, a reminder of how this one man's heroic act to save an unhatched egg multiplied into a lifetime of conservation activities that extended far beyond the avian world. Since then, Sandhill Cranes have been taken off the Endangered Species list. In fact, the pendulum has swung so far the other way that the International Crane Foundation in Baraboo, Wisconsin, is working to crane damage to corn and other crops. Otherwise, conflicts with farmers will grow.

All the more reason to read this book. We need *Sandy*, the memoir, we need Sandy, the bird, and we need more unsung, irresistible, bird-crazed heroes like Hyde. It is a pleasure to re-introduce this fine book.

Gretel Ehrlich
1999

Publisher's Note

Birdwatchers may note that some of the common names of birds used in the book are no longer in use. We have chosen to retain the nomenclature of the original edition.

CHAPTER

1

A lusterless, cold, gray dawn breaks on the spring damp of the marshy Oregon meadow; a cluster of white-faced Hereford cows, hair dull and lifeless from a long winter on hay, pull at the washy spring grass. From the dead rushes, a few motley blackbirds call halfheartedly as though in doubt of spring. Their voices are nervous, harsh, brittle; their feathers patchy and ragged. Something seems missing; something seems wrong.

I am a man too easily affected by the moods of nature, a cattle rancher, steeped in the old traditions of the West, yet with head and heart filled with wildlife—one given to restless dreams, clinging hopefully to nature as she is, relishing what has been, dreading what is in her future. My eyes burn, not from watching the grazing cattle, but from staring into the skies for signs of migrating Sandhill Cranes, those great marsh-dwelling birds so much a part of the sound and scene of the old West. They are late this year. Why haven't they come?

Tardy as they are, I have faith that they will come—this year, at least, and the next, and, perhaps, five years hence. But beyond that, who can say? Perhaps by then, when migrating flocks come winging in, there will be no ducks, no geese, no Sandhill Cranes, no Western Tanagers, only harsh, chattering hordes of super-efficient Starlings. The trends are already showing; there are ominous signs of decline among many species. But there is hope, too, for there is a subtle stirring among a few people who refuse to accept a "silent spring" as inevitable, people who, like myself, believe that the darkest shadow over the future of our wildlife heritage is our own complacency. Sandy is the story of one man's faltering steps, a tiny, cockeyed counterrevolution against despair to save an endangered species.

High above me as I write this, a Bald Eagle, head and tail glistening white as the feathers ruffle before a freshening breeze, wings bent sharply back like the imprint on a Navaho rug, swoops suddenly downward half a thousand feet, then, playfully, soars high again. I watch him as long as I can see him, caressing him with my look, until he passes beyond the ridges and is lost over the next valley. Whenever I see an eagle now, I watch until he is gone, for I am heavy with the sense that I may be seeing an eagle for the last time.

Klamath County, in southern Oregon, was once one of the great eagle ranges. When my uncle came here over half a century ago, there were thousands. Now, by the latest Fish and Wildlife Service survey, there are scarcely more than fourteen and only one of these an immature. The eagle is but one of the species dying out; there are others in trouble, such as the White Pelicans or my beloved Greater Sandhill Cranes.

My devotion to the cranes goes back over seventeen years, and it all started quite by accident with a chance tale by one of the cowboys with whom I worked. Roy, a wrinkled old Chetco Indian, was a man of many words, and he punctuated this garrulous flow with habitual, though gentle, profanity. Born in a coastal Indian village, he had drifted eastward fifty years before to the cattle country of southern Oregon. He was old when I first knew him, but his brown, short-fingered hands somehow helped shape my fate.

My eldest brother, Ted, had a large ranch in the Bly Valley, in Klamath County, a cow outfit, tougher and more tradition steeped than most. For a time, while I let my education digest and my marriage begin, old Roy and I were buckaroos together.

As a cowboy, I was unique in the intensity of concentration on the cattle business with which I started my day. I was intense often for a matter of minutes—until the first Green-tailed Towhee mewed in the sagebrush, the first Sandhill Crane goohrahed lonely from the awakening marshes, or a somber Townsend's Solitaire called from the blue-berried greenery of a juniper. To put it mildly, my brother, for whom I worked, was a very patient man.

While the old Indian constantly diluted my attention to my work with nature lore and oddments of the old West, it was his casual tale at supper one evening that shattered my peaceful existence. I remember that evening well—tired cowboys, faces poker straight over their plates, pensive, politely silent, save for the never faltering Roy, who murmured on and on like a quiet brook, scarce listened to, undemanding, black eyes sparkling with constant and easy good humor, always a gentle part of the background noises.

"Bigawd," he said, sipping away at his mug. "I shore saw somethin' today. I was ridin' over along the South Fork of the Sprague lookin' for a tight-bagged cow, and there was an old Sandhill Crane hen got her nest built square in the middle of the river." He stared for a moment into the black crystal ball of his coffee as though conjuring up an image, then went on. "Laid her old head straight out over the rushin' water and pretended she wasn't there, so, shucks, I looked straight ahead and pretended she wasn't there either, and rode on about my business." He poured himself another cup of black coffee, sugared it heavily, and resumed his narrative. "Shore is a shame."

My attention wandered loyally back to him. "What's a shame?" I asked.

"Why, that crane, of course. That old hen done a lot of work buildin' her a floatin' nest of rushes right out there in the water where it's safe from varmints, but she made one big mistake. She hooked it in the barbed wire of the fence where it crosses the channel, and when the South Fork rises in flood her nest will go plumb under."

My brother fixed the Indian with a cold stare. "Now what did you have to tell him that for? He'll hatch those eggs out in his bed, and I won't get any work out of him."

My thoughts roared into high gear, and I was off. "It might just work at that," I said. "My wife could sit on them during the day, and I could take the night shift."

Someone laughed nervously.

"It was but an idle jest," I said, looking about me at a host of disapproving eyes.

That night, as unheralded as the first robin, the spring rains came, melting the high snows on Gearhart Mountain, turning the rocky clay flats of the Fishhole country into a muddy morass. Slowly, the South Fork began to rise and to grow angrier. Under the eaves of my little house in Bly, throughout the long night, the water sputtered from the gutters, while the encroaching snowbanks retreated, exposing the stale mustiness of winter-moulded lawn. In the chill of the bedroom, I stood at the window and watched for dawn, pictured the nesting crane, wet and bedraggled on her floating island, the once placid river raging now, tearing at the bulk of resisting reeds, and she, uncomprehending, pressing the two big, hot, brown-mottled eggs to the tattered feathers of her breast.

At the first cold gray hint of dawn I left my wife to her lonely breakfast, pressed out into the slanting rain, and drove across the flooding valley to the ranch. Leaving my car, I splashed down across the wet meadows, the only sounds the sucking of my feet in the bogs, the plash of rain driving wave after wave across the puddles, the frightened piping of a Savannah Sparrow, skulking wet winged from one grass clump to another, and afar the first angry ratcheting warning of a male Sandhill Crane announcing my approach to his mate.

My hopes faded fast as I neared the bank of the South Fork where Roy had seen the nest. There was only a sullen, white-capped torrent where the nest had been, and a few barbed wires stretched taut, humming an off-keyed whine with the moaning, driving water. And yet, as I approached, there was something causing a backwash as it resisted the unrelenting surge, a small, tule-rush remnant of what had been, perhaps, a nest.

And then I saw her, a Sandhill Crane hen, half submerged in the rushing sea, feathers driven askew by the current, silver gray against the clay brown of the river, eyes bewildered but determined, ready to go down with her nest. Her red forehead was dulled with cold, limbs stiff, neck braced awkwardly against a strand of barbed wire for support, strength almost gone. I had only seconds to act; already her great yellow eyes were half closed, her life ebbing fast, and only instinct was keeping her from being swept away with her nest.

Shaking with the cold, I jerked my clothes off, dropped them on a clean patch of snow. The torrent swirled angrily about my legs, my hips, my chest, sucking away my breath, then, suddenly, even the ooze of the bottom, which had somehow anchored and reassured me, was gone, and I was swept helplessly numb out into the raging water. An angry wave of ice water crashing over my head brought me to my senses. "You damned bird-crazy fool," I thought bitterly. "What are you trying to do, anyhow?" But it was too late to change my mind.

Clutching a passing cake of ice, I held for a moment, trying to rest as the current whirled my body about and swept me down towards the nest. With a strange hiss and croak of anger the sandhill hen tried to defend her treasures, but as she flapped a wing, the nest suddenly began to disintegrate, and she was swept under.

Barbed wire tore at my hair as I caught at the lurching eggs with one desperate lunge. Crying out in excitement at feeling the big smooth globes in my hands, my mouth filled with muddy water. Instants later the nest was gone. My legs cramped as a great slanting cake of ice churned over me and drove me under. Far downstream as I sputtered up, I saw a flash as the hen's wing, stiffened by the cold, broke from the water in one last desperate flap, and then was gone forever.

Kicking hard for shore, eggs still clutched tightly in my hands, I fought helplessly against the surge. There was a stabbing pain in my back as a Medusa's head of driftwood smashed against me and was gone. Hampered by my plunder, I hooked myself up the bank with my elbows the way a sea elephant uses his flippers and lay there gasping. From somewhere in the mists, the sandhill's mate called sadly, hoping for an answer that would never come. Then, suddenly, great wings were over me as the male, beating hard against the winds and rain, dropped from the sky, its strident voice losing its sadness for anger and alarm. Desperately it crouched, feigning injury, trying to lure me away from the stream. Both its long wing plumes and short, square tail feathers were muddy and bedraggled.

Glancing down at the mottled brown eggs in my hand, I felt for one fleeting moment a terrible guilt and shame. Forgetting myself, I called softly to his anger. "Forgive me, bird. I am trying to help!"

Numbed by the cold, I dressed hurriedly and pressed the eggs against my stomach. Feeling their touch against my bare skin, I sensed from the temperature that one was cold and dead—indeed, perhaps it had never lived—but the other gave off a faint flickering of warmth and, in that warmth, life.

Halfway to the car, I paused and listened. Only the sound of rain skipping across endless puddles, and the far-off roar of angry waters; the old male had ceased for a time his lonely, heart-tugging call. I clutched both eggs carefully to the growing warmth of my stomach, and half an hour later they were soaking up heat in an incubator in my cosy little house in the town of Bly, while I fought off pneumonia in a hot bathtub.

CHAPTER

2

In those days the little town of Bly was a rough, tough logging and ranching town, affectionately dubbed "Little Rock on the Sprague" by its few native-born Oregonians. Nestled as it was against the Klamath Indian Reservation, it caught the renegades of both worlds—the Indians who, forbidden alcohol by law, bought shaving lotion by the case to drink in dark alleys, and the whites who made an illegal and ill-begotten livelihood bootlegging this perfumed hooch to them. In the summer, the logging industry—and thus the town—boomed; in the winter, the mills shut down, and the population huddled in their shacks, nursing their pot-bellied stoves, dodging creditors, watching half bemused as the merchants from the big city of Klamath Falls, fifty miles to the west, came to repossess automobiles and television sets and the law patrolled the streets and back alleys looking for scraps of illegal venison. Birds wild or tame could only be appreciated if edible, and the townspeople could readily forgive all sins but bird watching.

Horses wandered at will through everyone's yard, summering on flowers and vegetables and wintering on shrubbery. More than once, main-street traffic was held up for blocks by a stallion courting a mare in the middle of State Highway 66.

In the midst of all this chaos, the Bly ladies of the gardening society bustled about, overdressed and ever enthused, its various committees either running off the women of questionable virtue who set up some sort of hospitality center on Ivory Pine Road or making educational forays to explain the birds and the bees to the younger generation, whose experiences often involved a knowledge of more life than any of the ladies even dreamed existed.

The youth of the town, when not watching haircuts, strolled up and down the Appian Way of Highway 66, hoping that something exciting would happen, afraid to miss one single beat in the pulse of the town, wishing, as one gangling youth put it, "that somebody'll come along and give me a ride sommaires."

It was to this madcap pastoral scene that I brought my urban, California bride to dwell and bear our first son. Gerdi, my bride, was soon immersed in the town's affairs, and, in the first weeks following our "chivaree," attended no less than three combination wedding and baby showers, the brides, from thirteen to fifteen, standing a good chance of being grandmothers by the time they were twenty and seven.

However helpful her background of horses, the sheer, raw, blustering vitality of the Bly country was a little overpowering. And yet how hard she tried to enter into its spirit and tradition. She sent away for some material for a dress—beautiful material, with half the historic cattle brands of the old West printed gaily upon it. For days she sewed away and was wearing the dress in triumph down the main street of Bly when some old cowboy fresh off the Oregon desert nickered audibly as she breezed by, "Lookit the brands on that silly heifer. She shore must have changed hands a lot of times."

She soon acquired a troop of Campfire Girls, shy brown Indian girls, lovely as deer, who spent a great deal of time giggling in the bathroom as they flushed and reflushed the toilet with the greatest of wonderment.

Of our neighbors, one had lost a leg in an attempted robbery, another, along with bootlegging, ran a sort of way station for on-the-lam gangsters from the Middle West. Every few weeks, a big, black Lincoln would drive down the muddy streets, discharge some suspicious-looking characters into the unpainted shacks, stay for a few days until the heat was off, and depart. It was not until one of these temporary guests held up the local grocery store and made a dramatic but ill-concealed getaway by skirting the open fields about town straight to my neighbor's house that the local law was embarrassed to the point of cracking down.

Once there was a lull for some time in the various town activities until another neighbor was caught early one morning dragging a stolen safe down the road behind his pickup and was duly convicted and sent to the penitentiary.

I had a collection of birds on an acre or two hidden behind a board fence, which I built to screen my activities. One day as I was on my hands and knees planting a multiflora rose hedge, I heard my neighbor's boy inquire, "Dayaddy, whut awl cahned uv en ayakccent do Mistuh Hyad hev?"

It took me some time to realize that I in my bird-loving ways was even stranger to my neighbors than they were to me, and I am sure that they would have sent for the men in white coats if they had known about my home-made incubator coddling its two precious crane eggs.

Weeks went by before it became obvious that one of the eggs was never going to hatch, but, miracle of miracles, in spite of what it had been through, the second egg contained life. It was a lovely egg—a creation—a masterpiece, mottled with soft

browns and greens, as though each of the various marsh grasses among which the cranes fed had contributed a color. I was almost disappointed to see its perfection burst asunder—and totally unprepared to be the father of a Sandhill Crane.

First came a small hole about the size of a pencil, in the larger end of the egg. The small, rubbery orange beak that poked through looked inadequate for such a tough job, but then I noticed it was capped with a white egg tooth, which is nature's key to the eggshell prison and which disappears after the first few days of life. As the hole widened slowly, I saw the inner membrane of the egg, angry with exposed veins, discolored with stale juices, moist, fragile, drying to a brown, parchmented paper. The tappings of the weak chick seemed useless, ineffectual, but slowly the hole grew and became not a hole but a trench encircling the cap, which then fell away. For a time, the bird rested from its labors, seemed almost to have given up the struggle after this first small success. Then, movement again as I waited breathlessly. The neck uncoiled, the shell cracked asunder, and the wet, bedraggled chick flopped from its own puddling wastes and left the bloody shell behind. All the king's horses and all the king's men couldn't now undo what that tiny egg tooth had done.

It was my bride who brought me to my senses. "It's cute," she said, trying to be pleasant, "but what does it eat?"

I made a mad dash to the county library, sixty miles away, expecting all my problems to be miraculously solved, only to find that there is no big, definitive volume on the care and feeding of Sandhill Cranes. Wasting no more time on that fruitless adventure, I returned to Bly, grabbed a shovel, scraped away the remaining snow from the garden and began to dig, an action that attracted quite a crowd of the citizenry.

"Season open yet?" someone asked.

"Nope."

"'Pears you're goin' fishin'."

"Nope."

"Whatchall gonna dew, eat them worms for supper?"

I quit answering, kept digging.

Under the heat lamp in the kitchen, a fawn-colored Sandhill Crane chick, no longer wet and ugly, looking somewhat like a brown-eyed gosling, wobbled on shaky, orange legs and peeped incessantly. From the time the bird had rolled from the shell, I had offered him food, but the youngster refused to eat, and I thought ahead to the slow torture of helplessly watching it starve to death. Had I known more about cranes, I should have realized that during these first two days, when the remnants of the yolk sac are being absorbed, baby cranes are not at all interested in taking on food.

For a long day and night I spent a tender vigil at its side. Now and then the chick would reach down, take a good healthy grip on one wormlike toe, and flip itself over on its back, but it only peeped the louder and looked confused when I offered it a worm.

Sometimes it would cock its head and look up at me expectantly with dark brown, mysterious eyes, but for all my frantic and loving ministerings, it ate not. Weaker and weaker it seemed. Tiny, fragile, stretching out for long moments under the warmth of the heat lamp, hardly breathing, its peeping ever more feeble.

And then, somewhere in the cold dawn, the chick reached out suddenly, took a crushed worm from my fingers and swallowed it.

Shouting, I dashed into the bedroom. "It ate! It ate!"

"You woke the baby!" my wife said.

In the early hours of morning, the phone rang angrily. "I haven't seen you for a couple of days," my brother said.

"I've got quite a problem," I replied. "Another mouth to feed."

"You might try solving the problem by working," he suggested.

"I can't! It's that Sandhill Crane egg. It's hatched. Can't talk any longer; have to go now to feed—" But he had already hung up.

When I returned to the living room, my wife was on her hands and knees scrubbing her new rug. "Out, out, damned spot," she said, scowling. It seemed that the baby crane had followed me into the living room and had wasted a bomb on the rug.

In the end, threatened with eventual starvation, I had to return to work, and my wife accepted her lot quite stoically.

"You have to crush the worms," I said.

"Crush the worms?! Why?"

"I tried not. They go down the hatch almost eager to meet their doom, but once down there they change their mind and crawl right back out. And besides that they give Sandy a bellyache."

I owe a lot to Gerdi. She crushed the worms. As a matter of fact, she also dug the worms, for I was suddenly doing penance at the ranch.

* * *

By the time she was two weeks old, Sandy's appetite was voracious; she consumed large quantities of crushed worms and raw liver, as well as pheasant crumbles and such insects as I could collect for her in the still-cold marshes. Watching the liver go down was an oddity, for a large lump would be visible on the

left side of the neck. Descending the tube slowly, it would reach the middle of the long neck, cross over, and then descend the rest of the way on the other side.

Her legs had grown so rapidly that she was now like a gosling on stilts. Her devotion to us was pathetic—she had to be with Gerdi or myself, following us about, keeping us under constant surveillance, never more happy than when tugging on the nap of the rug at our feet with her rubbery beak. At times she would stretch out contentedly under the heat lamp, but the slightest hint of footsteps would bring her running, beak outstretched, for a handout. Any crumb that fell from our son's highchair was instantly devoured with shrill pipings for more, and young Dayton soon found it was much more fun to shove food over the edge to Sandy than to eat it himself.

What pessimists we were. We kept expecting the bird to die. From my childhood I had raised all manner of wild things, done everything from falconry and rescuing flooded waterfowl nests to setting the broken leg of a wounded bullfrog, but raising a complicated young Sandhill Crane seemed too much of a challenge.

For one thing, the Sandhill Crane in the wild is a bird of loneliness, frequenting the sequestered marshes wherever people have not made too much of an inroad. While their great rolling voices carry afar from the marshes or from the upper limits of the heavens they fly, the cranes themselves are most secretive, keeping well back from roads in breeding season and avoiding our usual paths. Their sounds are part of the undercurrent of spring and, unless one pauses to listen, are seldom noticed. It was thus that many a rough, tough old Bly logger who had spent his lifetime within hearing distance of the cranes, looked over our garden fence with an amazed "Now what kind of a critter is that?"

However much our feeding program was by guess and by gosh, Sandy not only prospered but was obviously as flourishing a specimen as could be produced in the wild. But one great problem haunted us and was to shadow poor Sandy to the end of her days. She did not realize that she was not one of us, and those other cranes with whom she might have had joyous consort were ever far beneath her.

CHAPTER

3

As summer approached, Sandy's feathers pushed through the soft buff down and through the blue-black of the blood-heavy quills. As if by magic, day by day she was transformed into an ungainly young lady. While her father and mother had possessed bare foreheads of brilliant, rose skin, hers was as yet feathered and would be so until the following February, when the feathers would begin to rub away, exposing more and more of the caruncular red of maturity. Then, too, would the infant piping give way to the croak of the adult, rusty, faltering, and inept, at first, then proud, stentorian, and musical, challenging the world.

Hers was the command now of Dayton's plastic wading pool, where she delighted in turning his merry baths into complete chaos. If Dayton splashed her, she splashed delightedly back. Then, when she had had enough, she would stand back contentedly, peeping in happiness, preening the flaking itch from her clean new feathers.

The wing feathers nearest her body as she stood with wings outstretched were developing into plumes. Her tail was actually short and square like that of a Canada Goose, but when she folded her wings, those wing plumes draped elegantly behind her as though part of the tail. No longer was she a little bird; she was a stately and imposing empress, some five feet tall with a wingspread of over six feet. She had become a crane in everything but her concept of herself—which was, of course, that she was a human. In her we perceived the same habits and patterns of the wild, the same dance steps, the same voice, and vocabulary, the same habits of probing the ground with her long beak, bowing to greet a friend, body laterally compressed, voice guttural, head low. Soon she was spreading her long wings against the fingerings of the winds, caught up by the instinct of flight, making short runs along the ground and long broadjumps, after which she would puff up her feathers, bow her head to the ground, and purr contentedly with a deep, throaty growl.

If I consented to share this with her she was delighted. It must have been a strange sight indeed for the people of Bly, for I would spread my arms, flap them like wings, and Sandy would croak with delight and follow suit, round and round the garden, over the back fence, out over the hot summer fields. When, lungs bursting, I would stop to look about, the curtains of the

neighboring houses would flutter as faces quickly retreated. Once one of the neighbors got to not watching so hard he shingled himself right off his roof, sending mud, garbage, shingles, and nails splattering in all directions.

And then one day, catching a sudden gust of wind, Sandy became accidentally and irretrievably airborne. With a squawk of mingled terror and delight, she sailed high and uncertainly out over the town. On one end of Bly she used the towering cloud of mill smoke as a pylon for her racing turn, then the church spire for another. At this proud moment in her history, she was sailing gracefully when her thoughts seemed suddenly to catch up with her—and especially an awareness that I was no longer with her. With a whoop that brought housewives rushing out into their yards, she headed pell-mell for home.

It was unfortunate that at this moment one of my neighbors, in a high condition of inebriation, was also navigating homeward. This was always accomplished by a tender ritual on the part of the bartender, who would lead him out to the center line of Highway 66 in front of the bar, show him the white line, and give him a gentle push in the direction of home. With this initial momentum, and a delicate perpetuating balance between leaning forward and falling, he would lurch forward and homeward. His wife would watch for him out the front window, and as he staggered down the white line past the house she would collar him and drag him in. It always worked with fair precision, except when the wags in town would turn him about and he would find himself, on sobering, miles from town and headed east for Lakeview.

On that fateful first flight of Sandy's, as the drunk was white-lining it past my house on his way home, Sandy chose to attempt a highway landing behind the man. Hearing the cry and the hissing beat of wings, the man glanced over his shoulder, cried out hysterically, and tried to run. If it was Sandy's first attempt at landing, it was also the drunk's first attempt at outrunning a Sandhill Crane, and both were doomed to disaster.

Overshooting her mark, she swept onward to a direct hit against the fleeing man. I ran to help, but it was too late. The sprinter had already somersaulted down over the embankment, landed face first in the red mud of the borrow pit, and had either fainted with terror or passed out. Flushed with the triumph of her first solo flight, Sandy flapped her wings to smooth her disheveled feathers, tipped her head back to the skies, and uttered a challenging squawk of pride.

From that day on, flying became Sandy's joy. I cannot truthfully call it her great abiding passion, because her great abiding passion was me. But she loved to buzz the town, looking for all the world like some great prehistoric bird, eons back in time, neck outstretched, downbeat slow, measured, graceful, upbeat quick, but almost reluctant, as though for that split instant she almost dared to fall. In the quiet summer evenings when the mill smoke hung lazily in the tepid air, she would make her final house count of the town before surrendering it to the birds of darkness, a brief circle about the house and back lot for height, then off on her beloved course, far down around the mill smoke to the west, then back around the town and church spire to the east.

Perhaps because I could not follow her, she took the skies as belonging peculiarly to her, cocking an eye skywards and croaking angrily at any interloper, whether a Violet- green Swallow or a giant airliner. For planes with their angry drone she held a lifetime hatred and would tip her head back and challenge them with full voice, long before they came into the range of human hearing and long after they had crashed into the horizon. Often when a plane appeared in the heavens, this self-appointed menace to navigation would mount the thermals and attempt to escort the plane out of her territory, but, fortunately for the pilots, she never quite understood the speed of those saucy demons of the air. By the time she had gained a thousand feet of elevation, they would be retreating in terror over the horizon, and she would settle comfortably to earth, smug with the satisfaction that she had protected her family and driven the enemy from the scene.

Sandy came to know when it was time for Dayton to come out to play. Peering intently through the windows, she would

wait for him on the front porch, piping excitedly when some movement from within gave a hint that he might come. Once he was out, she was perfectly content, staying beside him as he played—Dayton, playing in the sand, aware of the taboos of his mother's garden; Sandy, aware, I'm sure, but not caring, pulling up all my wife's bulbs with her great probing bill and laying them in tender homage at Dayton's pudgy feet.

In the night, she kept her attendant vigil on the front porch, watching us through the glass, sorrowful at her exclusion, catching the great moths as they fluttered against the panes and shredding their powdery wings on the front steps. From time to time she would purr quietly to us through the glass some Sandhill Crane devotion only she could understand. Somehow the whole house slept the better for having her there to guard against the evils of the night. All the time she was there, we were never once attacked by bandits, Indians, or traveling salesmen.

A highly social bird, Sandy's great craving was for companionship, pure and simple. There is nothing more pathetically lonely than a single Sandhill Crane, for by the very essence of their nature they are gregarious, except for that brief interlude in the year when they are nesting and become highly territorial. Even then, when the male is off feeding alone and the female attends to wifely duties, they will occasionally call to each other over the marshes, as though each wished to reassure the other of their presence and loyalty.

Nothing pleased Sandy more than an outing with her human friends. Brimming with excitement, garrulous, ready to bounce and dance, she would flap her wings excitedly, begging me to fly with her. Flying ahead a short distance, pre-guessing and checking out my route, she would probe for food with her nervous bill until I caught up, then charge off again. Sometimes she would spot something afar and fly off independently to investigate it, looking, suddenly, quite primitive and out of the past, a huge pterodactyl, a startling hangover from the Mesozoic era of geologic time. Watching her, my flesh would crawl with excitement as though I were projected back into the past and unable to return. I would imagine I was a primitive man, afraid his own shadow might jump him, ever watchful of the sky and ground for the approach of danger. Carried away by the stark reality of the scene, I would step suddenly into a thicket and immediately breathe easier. But then the pterodactyl, now a mere speck in the sky, would become slowly and immeasurably bigger, and bigger, and bigger, wings spread wide, primaries gaping to let slip the wind, swooping on helpless prey, dead on target, the brush no longer protective but grossly inadequate, and I, exposed as though I stood upright in sacrifice on an empty plain.

There is in a Sandhill Crane no movement, no action not of immaculate grace, unless it is at that moment when they first touch land from flight. But then, once settled, they are pure grace again with elegant and measured step, as though that one ungainly moment had never been. Since people first tried to reproduce the beauty of their world upon a cavern wall, the cranes have fascinated them, and they have sought to capture their plumed elegance. But their grace is also one of movement, more than faultless line, a dignity, a balance, and a poise.

How many people have stood like me but eons back in time and watched the dancing of the Sandhill Cranes, stood and wondered at the ritual of the dance, the bowing, leaping, tossing sticks in the air, calling to each other in high excitement? Was it the sandhill, perhaps, who first taught primitive people to dance? Was not so much ritual in a bird, to the primitive mind, something of the supernatural?

And imagine the effect of the great yellow sandhill eyes, unblinking, seen head on, cornered and hissing in fear, head

and neck like a reptile poised to strike, its gaze piercing straight to a person's soul. Try to outstare it, and the gaze impales you, frightens you with its knowledge of things deep, things mysterious, things of the future, and things of the far away and long ago. An eternal wisdom there, greater, older infinitely than ours—an amazing eye into which one reads all things. Laughter there, perhaps, or is it anger? Always pride, and once in Sandy's later years, sorrow and shame.

There was friendship in her eye, too, and quiet adoration. Often of a quiet evening I used to sit with my family on the front porch at Bly and listen for the far-off calling of cranes on the distant marshes, talking to Sandy in a gentle, easy voice, until she flopped contentedly beside us. I would tell her then of Yamsi, a wonderful valley to the north, where I grew up—a land of mountain meadows, clear water, and pine trees. Yamsi, headwaters of the Williamson, cattle and wildlife paradise—since first I saw it as a young boy, I had walked in a constant dream that some day my uncle who owned the ranch would let me take over there. Sandy could not grasp the words, of course, but how quickly she would sense my mood and mirror my sadness or excitement.

My marriage had been conditional on the agreement that whatever the primitive life to which I subjected my wife, Gerdi, we would always return to Palo Alto, California, for Christmas. There were some tense moments that fall, when we tried to agree on what to do with Sandy, for, while we might have farmed out a couple of children, no one was about to put up with a confounded Sandhill Crane. In the end, Sandy went right along, flopped in my wife's lap in the front seat, enjoying every moment of her trip as though she had suddenly discovered a soft, crazy way to migrate south for the winter without working at it, delighted in watching the scenery float by without the slightest effort on her part. With her high center of gravity and long legs she soon learned that it was far better to stay crouched than to have to ride out the curves while standing.

But with Sandy adventure was never very far away. Stopped by a gruff-voiced state policeman for a hair crack in our taillight, we had almost visited our way out of the predicament with only a warning, when the policeman bent forward to catch my embarrassed mumbling. Sensing drama, Sandy flashed out protectively with her stabbing bayonet of a beak and grabbed the man by the ear lobe. If the Irish have a sense of adventure, we didn't discover it that day.

Time has a way of slipping by unnoticed. Sandy grew, as did the size of my family, for when Sandy was a year-and-a-half old we added my daughter Ginny. Poor Sandy came to realize that whenever we trotted out the bassinet again she was in for a few months of neglect.

By her second year Sandy had achieved a stature nothing short of magnificent, with lovely, soft gray plumage, forehead of bright rose caruncles, and a voice that could be heard halfway to the moon. She hated loud, sharp noises other than those she produced herself, and by tapping my knife handle against wood I could cue her into tipping her head back like some dowdy opera star, opening her great beak to the heavens, half-closing her great yellow eyes, and crashing forth with a massive and staccato squawk.

It was on one of those Christmas trips south with Sandy that we passed a restaurant and watering place known as "Bill and Kathy's," in Dunnigan, California. It so happened that the new bartender there had recently been on the road as a fire extinguisher salesman, and, having dropped by the ranch in Oregon, had been greatly impressed by Sandy and her vocal powers. Spotting my wife and me as we fed and watered Dayton and Ginny, he came rushing over to ask about his feathered friend, and, learning that none other was waiting out in the car, he brightened immediately.

"Say," he said. "Would you do me a big favor?" I felt faint stirrings of misgivings but I nodded. "There's a drunk in the bar, and I'm having quite a time getting him to go home. Maybe if you—." The whole plan crashed suddenly into place.

While the bartender returned to his bar, I paid my check and sauntered to the car. I held the door open for Sandy, who stepped casually out on the sidewalk, flapped her wings noisily, by way of stretching, preened an errant feather or two, then followed me nonchalantly into the open door of the bar. Solemnly, I sat down on a stool, while Sandy stepped up beside me. There was a stark stillness in the whole room as I said, "Give me and my old friend here a drink—like maybe a straight shot of vodka."

"Coming up," the bartender replied, sliding out two glasses and filling them with water poured from a vodka bottle.

Sandy dipped her beak in the glass, drank thirstily with head tilted to the ceiling, then drank again. There was a rattling gasp from the corner of the room, as a big, moon-faced man pushed himself clumsily to his feet. "Whoosh!" he stammered.

As he sidled by, with malice aforethought I tapped the back of my knife on the edge of the bar. Sandy's great eyes sparkled yellow, her head went back in thunderous laughter, and while we covered our splitting eardrums in the resulting bedlam the drunk clutched his old hat down over his ears and fled into the street.

CHAPTER

4

To have known Sandy as I did, it was inevitable that I became a devout crane man. What had been published about cranes was meager indeed—too many gaps of knowledge and too many assumptions, which in the light of our life with Sandy seemed like errors. And then, as though to spur my affection and concern, of all the Bly Sandhill Cranes that migrated south that fall, less than half the population returned the following spring.

What happened to them I never discovered. But they were gone, and in my sorrow and alarm I took new stock of the situation. For the first time I looked on valleys that every spring since I had been a boy had been noisy with the lonely goohrahing of the cranes, and found them strangely silent. A thousand questions filled my mind. How old were sandhills when they mated and bred? What percentage of the usual clutch of two eggs hatched? How many of the young were able to elude predators, hunters, thoughtless boys with guns, rampaging storms, power lines, hunger, poisons, and insecticides to become breeding pairs? How much true nesting territory was actually left to them in the United States and Canada? What were their wintering problems? How strong their genetic components for survival? Were they, like their cousin the Whooping Crane, fast disappearing from their ranges? Were they dying out in other valleys besides my own?

And then I thought of what it would be like when they were all gone, their great voices stilled, no longer echoing over the marshes and the lonely wet meadows. Gone for all time, and no human miracle, no atomic wizardry, could bring them back. Only a few museum specimens would be left, gaunt and sterile in their glass cases, gathering dust and feeding the larvae of moths— gone like the great auk, the heath hen, the passenger pigeon, and a host of others. It would be as though springs and brooks had everywhere lost their gurgle, as though the pines had ceased their soughing and the wild geese their call. Surely so great a bird, so integral a part of the sights and sounds of the American frontier, deserved a chance.

My first impulse was to consult the Fish and Wildlife Service in Washington, but this proved unrewarding. The Service, limited as it was in funds, had to devote itself to those species that were hunted, such as ducks and geese. Perhaps there was some logic in this, since most of the funds for management come from the sale of duck stamps, but I had to reason also that there are really more wildlife lovers than hunters among the taxpayers and that surely the Greater Sandhill Crane deserved some interest, too.

"Quite frankly," an official told me, "we are not worried about the Sandhill Crane." And then, in a more kindly tone, he went on, "If you have questions about them, why don't you find out the answers yourself."

Taking time out from work, I threw myself into a crash program of getting some indication of the remnant population. That month most of the grocery money went for postage stamps, and report after report came in. Four hundred sandhills here, two fifty, a thousand—most reports of large groups of Sandhill Cranes turned out to be little brown, or lesser, sandhills on migration from the far north and not our native greater sandhills at all. The little brown is to the greater sandhill what the cackling goose is to the big Canadian honker. It is a much smaller bird, lacking the dignity and style of its huge cousin. The lesser nests

in the far north and thus, protected by the wilderness, numbers about one hundred thousand birds. Flocks of ten thousand are not uncommon due to the bird's gregarious nature, and a hunting season has been deemed necessary to ease its agricultural depredations.

However, the greater sandhill, whose nesting is mainly restricted to the fast disappearing marshes of the United States, is becoming a rare bird. It would be a shame if the similarity in appearance between the lesser and the greater caused the downfall of the superior bird, but this cousinship has added one more burden to an already overwhelming load. Here terminology is important. Science has by and large abandoned the term "little brown" favoring the term "lesser," but this has made the protection of the rare bird increasingly difficult. When hunting magazines now come out with recipes for cooking the hunted subspecies, they merely call them Sandhill Cranes. Less and less is the average American aware that the greater is a native bird needing every bit of protection it can get and that the hunted subspecies is only here as a migrant, a winter visitor from the far north.

In my studies I found that there were two main islands of population, in Oregon and in Michigan, with a few smaller populations scattered between. By writing letters, by relentless pursuit of biologists, and by hitching plane and helicopter rides over most of the known nesting marshes, I determined that in all the vastness of the United States there were less than three thousand Greater Sandhill Cranes. Of these many were nonbreeders, some too old, some too young to mate. Once a species declines too far in numbers, the end can come frighteningly fast.

The decline of the species became sharply evident, of course, right on my own doorstep. Only a year before I had sat on the front porch of my brother's ranch house in the Bly Valley and watched, at one time, four separate pairs with young. Now two of these pairs had vanished through the winter, not to return, and another female returned that tragic spring to wander forlorn and alone, faithful to the territory that had held her for years, scanning the skies from time to time and listening skyward for a mate who never came and was not destined to come again. What pairs were left I came to know more intimately than ever through the years, and they to know me, as though they sensed somehow that this strange, tall cowboy was their friend.

Sometimes, as we sat eating in the ranch dining room, one of the hands would say, "Saw a pair of sandhills today," in such and such a field, and I would reply, "Yes, a big reddish-gray male, pretty old, and the female agey too, with some feathers missing from the right wing. Raised one young last year and one this, but lost them both in migration."

There would be silence then, and I would feel a guilt that perhaps I knew more about cranes than I knew about my work. I would decide then and there that my mind would stay on things other than cranes, but then I would reason, "If I am not interested in them, who will be?" And by next morning, when Sandy would follow after me like a faithful friend to superintend my work, my mind would drift once more to the cranes and their problems, and my ears would be tuned to the meadows and the soft, hushed loneliness of the land for their distant calls.

CHAPTER

5

The spring of 1954 brought a partial fulfillment of my childhood dreams. It may have been that my brother was good and sick of hearing about Sandhill Cranes; at any rate, as manager of my uncle's land and cattle company, he sent me, with my growing family, some thirty-five miles northwest to manage Yamsi, the ranch on which I had spent my boyhood. My uncle had pioneered Yamsi, putting it together from a series of Indian claims. Eventually the ranch became headquarters for his corporation, known as the Yamsay Land and Cattle Company, or the Bar Y.

Some ten miles long, Yamsi contained the valley of the headwaters of the Williamson River, a lovely, quiet, crystalline stream welling from the base of a great pumice-covered ridge, meandering north amongst grassy meadows rimmed with lodgepole and ponderosa pine, growing larger and larger as it passed a number of contributory springs, and eventually—at least during summer months—all but disappearing on the vast Klamath Marsh, some fifty miles to the north.

In 1843, Fremont, the explorer, came to the valley from Klamath Marsh, turned up over the shoulder of Yamsay Mountain, at the north end of the ranch, then proceeded down Long Creek to the Sycan Marsh and eventually to the Oregon desert.

On either side of the ranch was a buffer zone of from thirty to a hundred miles of uninhabited forest, which gave the place the seclusion I loved. The trout fishing was magnificent, but best of all there was a marsh potential I would develop for waterfowl and cranes.

In 1928 my uncle hired an Italian cowboy, whose one distinction lay in the fact that he had once been apprenticed to a stonemason in Italy. Despairing of ever making a cowhand out of the man, my uncle pointed to a great natural outcropping of gray lava rock and said, "Joe, get the hell off that horse and go build me a house."

In those days, before the advent of logging trucks, logs were hauled out of the forest by railroads. Fortunately, one such railroad ran along the ridges of Yamsay Mountain, and my uncle was able to ship the lumber for his new edifice by rail from Klamath Falls. From the rail's end, some five miles back in the hills, the lumber wound its way down to the ranch by team and wagon. The lava rock, of course, split from surrounding rimrocks, was entirely local, as were the great brown natural logs of ponderosa pine that framed the windows and made the support columns of the porches.

However large it was, it blended beautifully with the surrounding rocks and pines. Whatever errors or aberrations there were in its design were not the fault of the Portland architect but a manifestation that the determination of my uncle was stronger than his. If it was built by cowboy labor, it still managed all the charm of a Swiss chalet. The rock work was so well done that the Italian never had to cowboy again, for he built many of the rock houses of the Klamath Falls area.

No house could have been better situated. Standing serenely tucked away in a bay at the head of the valley, it was embraced by great rolling ridges of virgin ponderosa pine, which shouldered away the encroaching winds. The large windows looked out upon pine trees and the shine of water, green

meadows yellow with buttercups, blue with wild iris and dainty but profuse penstemon. Beside the house ran a cold, placid stream, welling from the rocks, mirrorlike with the stark intensity of its reflections, finger numbing, even on the hottest days of summer. Thronged with bush willows in thick clumps, it was the haunt of Mallards and Cinnamon Teal on summer evenings. North across a log bridge lay barns and corrals and, beyond that through the pines, the headwaters of the Williamson River.

Oddly enough, no wild geese had nested here within the memory of the white settlers, but I soon changed all this. When I should have been helping my wife with all the complexities of moving, I was off gathering goose eggs from drowning nests in the Bly Valley, and these I rushed to Yamsi to hatch out. I knew that if they hatched out in my valley the goslings couldn't care less where they had been laid as eggs. These rescued eggs were accordingly hatched out under bantam hens, released on the ponds, and eventually became the progenitors of a nesting population that now numbers some fifty pairs.

Poor Gerdi. What a patient Griselda she was. If in every marriage there is one massive blunder on the part of the husband that is held over his head during every subsequent domestic hassle or cocktail-party soliloquy, then mine was this moving day. I have always studiously avoided teaching my wife the use of firearms, and this may be the reason I am alive today.

Even with fair warning, women walk blithely into marriage, secure in the knowledge that whatever the bad habits of the man, they can change all that. When we were being "chivareed" by the Bly folk on the occasion of our first night in our little house, we slipped out of our bedroom window through a prickly thicket of wild plum, tiptoed around in the darkness, and joined the group singing boisterously and with many a ribald comment at our door. The man ahead of us, a crusty old rancher named Basil Hall, turned to me over his shoulder and said, "Wonder why a nice girl like Gerdi would marry a blankety-blank like him."

Gerdi should have packed and run right then and there. However, we hustled everyone in with a show of hospitality and plied them with quantities of homemade chokecherry wine, which had long before turned to vinegar. Everyone got horribly ill, and I made sure Basil got sicker than anyone else.

Yet how right the man was. On that moving day, while I was off hip deep in the marshes rescuing goose eggs, Gerdi packed and moved all our belongings, loaded on a truck sixty mink cages I felt I had to have for setting hens, cooked three big meals, cleaned the house for sale, and plucked and butchered a hundred frying chickens and a hundred white Peking ducks. (I had this idea we should be self-supporting.) Whether or not I helped her load the washing machine and the freezer on the truck is a point I can't really remember. The way she tells it, she had our daughter Marsha that day, too, but I think it was a day or two later.

At Yamsi there was always a host of projects to keep us busy. Gerdi had the big stone house, a huge rock garden, and three young children, while I had the ranch operation, some fifteen hundred cattle, six thousand acres of deeded land, and a hundred thousand acres of Indian-reservation leased range. Sandy, accepting the move with good grace, took over as foreman.

She supervised everything, often with lusty comments that were usually sufficiently ill timed to disrupt whatever operation was taking place. In Sandy's decade at Yamsi, no one ever quite succeeded in corralling a steer or horse on the first try, for, dollars to doughnuts, whenever one would herd an animal forward toward the gate, Sandy somehow always knew and would come shuffling up from nowhere to defend the gate and block the way. There would be a ruffling of feathers as noisy as the riffling of a deck of cards in a church, the red forehead would tilt to the sky, and the heavens would fill with Sandy's deafening laughter. While the terrified animal would charge back underneath one's horse to escape to the woods, the sky would fill with the buckeroo smoke of profanity.

The situation would be especially acute in the autumn, when we would rise with the dawn, saddle our shivering horses, gather a bunch of fat steers for a buyer, and start them toward the scales for weighing. It was a nervous operation. Any loss of time, any running on the part of the steers would be readily translatable into losses of hundreds of dollars' worth of weight. Sandy, of course, would be locked in a shed, but invariably, just as the steers had allayed their suspicions enough to approach the corrals, Sandy would con one of the children into letting her out, and, wings beating dramatically, croaking gutturally for all Klamath County to hear, front and center would come that abominable bird, and the steers would break and run.

Loud as she shouted herself, she always objected strenuously to excess noise in others, so any loud blasphemy on my part during those awful moments only increased her racket, until one had to break the impasse by riding quietly away in disgust. Never has there been a fishwife who could out-cuss Sandy.

While quite fond of people, Sandy had a gentle but mischievous way of sidling up and, with long probing bill, untying people's shoes or taking the buttons off one's shirt or the rivets from one's Levis with a deft twist of her bill and swallowing them before they were missed. Nor could she let sleeping dogs lie, for she knew all the favorite hiding places of our English setter, Spray, and would sneak up on her as she dreamed of catching a squirrel, seize Spray's tail with her bill, and hang on for a crazy Nantucket sleigh ride.

I always wished that Spray, who could even kill a badger, would show more spunk and at least growl, but she would only get that "Must I endure this?" look in her sad brown eyes and slink away. She went to great extremes to outwit her tormenter. But wherever she hid, including the top of the haystack, she could only have a few minutes' peace, for, like an avenging angel, Sandy would appear, stalking her trail.

Her quarry once more routed, Sandy would puff up her feathers in satisfaction, flap her wings with a short triumphant rush, slide to a stop to stand on tiptoe as she bowed her head low, with beak almost touching the ground. Purring a low growl of delight, she would check to see if I was watching then once more set out on the poor dog's trail.

Gentle as she was with children, she had one definite—alas, violent—antipathy. In her long lifetime, she could not tolerate a strange woman wearing slacks. She would pretend to be minding her own business, but her crafty eyes would begin to sparkle with rage. She would circle, beak pointed downward, edging closer to the target while seeming to ignore it. Then, before I could intercept her, she would dart swiftly in to deliver a series of sharp stabs to the wallet pocket and hang on for dear life to her now hysterical victim. Occasionally, I found the situation acutely embarrassing; most of the time I felt a secret satisfaction bordering on triumph.

She treated Gerdi with the studied indifference of a wife for a mistress. Put bluntly, she actually snubbed her; if there were moments when she might have wondered what Gerdi's exact position was in my life, it could not have occurred to Sandy that she herself was not the mistress or lady of the house and Gerdi a mere servant who cooked the meals, raised the children, and could be cajoled at any hour into a handout. If Gerdi and I made the mistake of standing together in her presence, Sandy had a way of edging between us with the greatest dignity. It was a great blow to my wife's ego, however, that Sandy never really considered her serious competition.

There were probably storms between the two that I never glimpsed, for Gerdi was as avid a gardener as Sandy was a degardener, a puller-upper of bulbs and flowers. She would often slip up behind my wife as she was on her hands and knees planting a long row of strawberries, perhaps, and poor Gerdi would look back after an arduous hour kneeling at the altar of the soil to contemplate with satisfaction the results of her task, only to find that Sandy had taken the plants up, shaken the dirt off the roots, and laid them neatly beside the holes.

The electricity at the ranch being of our own making, it was never quite feasible to have a clothes dryer, and Gerdi always had a huge daily load of wash to hang out on the clothesline beside the house. There was something about a white sheet that Sandy could never resist. It was made to be stabbed with a muddy bill. Just as we branded our cattle, she never seemed to insist upon more than a simple trademark, and yet she was never satisfied until each unmarked piece of sheet or white service bore her brand.

There was always a difficult decision to make on dropping a clothespin—whether to bend over and expose oneself or take the chance of Sandy seizing the pin, spreading her wings, and whirling off for a game of toss on the meadows.

It was at about this stage in Sandy's life that I realized I was neglecting my wife and actually took her to a dance in town. At least we started those sixty miles. High up on the ridge top of ponderosa pine and manzanita brush, I caught a flash of gray among the trees. Chasing off in my best suit, I came back with a young Whistling Swan with a broken wing. Who can dance when a bird needs help? And so, Flatfoot, once his wing was mended, elected to enter the family and, even though joined by others of his kind for his frequent flights, stayed with us for many a year. In his loneliness, Flatfoot soon took up with Sandy, even began calling in unison with her in a call that changed day by day until it was an almost exact imitation of a Sandhill Crane's.

But Sandy loved him not. Blackbirds bothered Sandy constantly during the nesting season, as they do all sandhills. I once observed a wild male crane, pestered to the limit of his patience, leap into the air repeatedly, trying to stab the blackbirds scolding him from the branches with his long, sharp beak. Again and again the tormented crane leaped and struck, but the saucy birds flirted with him, just out of his reach. Sandy, with two or three blackbirds perching on her back, occasionally sidled past the swan in hopes of losing the blackbirds, but the ruse never seemed to work. At other times, even when the swan was calling its crane call in unison, Sandy ignored it completely.

Sandy was at home here at Yamsi, as were we all. For my wife and me life had suddenly ceased being a dream, and we clung to each departing day as something infinitely precious, never to be lived again.

CHAPTER

6

One evening, having put Dayton, Ginny, and Marsha to bed, my wife and I were sitting before a roaring pitch fire in the huge stone fireplace at Yamsi, while I was engaged in tweaking my wife's left ear in rapt adoration. There was a sudden squawk of jealous opprobrium from Sandy, who, as usual, was pacing her lonely vigil in the light-shafted darkness of the front porch, watching, as was her wont, in the front window.

"She ought to have a mate," I said.

"But the two of you make such a lovely couple," Gerdi replied, worming away from my caress and retreating to the end of the couch.

"Just the same, if anything should happen to me, I think she should have a mate of her own species."

And so, in time, we raised a mate for Sandy, hatching it, as we had Sandy, from a salvaged egg. The parents of this egg were Sycan Marsh birds of tremendous size, and I was eager to see what this mating would produce, because, to my knowledge, greater sandhills had never been bred in captivity. Since Sandy was undisputed queen of the ranch, and the male had a natural

reddish tinge, we named him the "Red King."

Cranes do not mate until they are three or four, so trying to interest him in the haughty dowager right away was a hopeless undertaking. We hoped that something would happen at two, for the Red King had developed into a magnificent specimen who stood chest high to a tall Indian. While he made a bulky nest of sticks and grasses at the shores of the pond in front of the house, he was stymied by the fact that Sandy had no realization that she was a Sandhill Crane and not a human. She was quite sociable with the King as long as I was out of sight and out of mind, but she obviously found me a far more fascinating fellow than the King. Whenever I hove into sight, she would immediately desert his side for mine, a fact that accounted, no doubt, to a great extent for Red King's vile temper.

Ill tempered he certainly was. He would wait until a person's back was turned, leap high in the air, and, with beak and sharp toenails, rip one's jacket to shreds.

His pet victim was a one-armed hay hauler named Louie, who, hearing noises in the willows one day, left his hay truck to investigate and walked right in on Red King's special territory, a secluded watering hole amongst the willows at the edge of the spring. Had Louie stood his ground, everything would have been all right, but the sight of a huge, unknown species of prehistoric bird with long, sharp beak screaming at him from five feet so unnerved Louie that he fled with the Red King in hot pursuit. At one point he tripped in a slough and lost half his shirt to the

crane before he managed to squirm away. Jumping into his truck, he crashed it into gear, jerked it forward to scatter the hay load all over the lot, then roared off down the road without even bothering to collect his pay.

The King was not at this time without competition for Sandy's favor, for I was, by now, on fairly intimate terms with some wild cranes. On migrating north the previous spring, they had been trapped by unseasonably heavy spring snows and had found that I was a soft touch for groceries. Henceforth, seeing me often in the company of Sandy and the Red King, they more or less accepted me as part of the local scene. As faithful as she was to me, I liked to think that it was greatly against her will that she became *enceinte*. Not wishing to trouble her with the burden of sitting on some obviously infertile eggs, I gathered her first two big, mottled treasures from a shallow scoop in the calf pasture and set them out, from force of habit, under a bantam. But three weeks later, not to be outwitted, Sandy laid two more eggs as lovely as the first. Again I set them under a bantam.

I made a big mistake, however, letting her off so easily from the duties and responsibilities of motherhood, for the first eggs hatched, and, just as I had reached the breaking point, playing foster mother to two young sandhill babies, the second two hatched, and the battle was on.

In vain I tried to interest Sandy in taking over at least part of her duties, but she had a way of staring at me, quite absorbed in what I was trying to show her, then turning quietly and, with a staged sort of dignity, walking off and leaving me to my work. Everything else I did, she had to supervise, but not this. While Sandy became more than ever a lady of leisure, I became a digger of earthworms, a slicer of wet, raw liver, a referee between little roughnecks, a procurer for insatiable gourmands, a father, a mother, a psychoanalyst for the emotionally unstable, and just plain slave, servant, and fall guy.

While the ranch business went to pot, the young hoodlums flourished. I soon found, however, that I couldn't raise the young ones together but had to give each a foster mother of their very own. If two were together, all might go well for some weeks, but suddenly one or the other of them would get in a good solid peck, and the other would flee in headlong retreat, battling any obstacles that kept it from fleeing its adversary.

I was to raise many cranes in later years, but I found this to be consistently a problem, and never was I destined to raise two together under a single foster mother. It appeared to be a matter neither of sexual difference nor of size, for often it was the smaller, later-hatched chick of a pair of nestmates that got in the telling punch. Given complete freedom to flee in such a perturbed state, the young birds went great distances, through streams, marshes, and forest, obviously with no intention of returning to the foster mothers to whom they were apparently devoted. I followed them, of course, and brought them back, but it was as though they had made up their tiny minds toward some sort of avian suicide, and it took much attention and quiet soothing on my part to calm them down.

In the wild, there seem to be a preponderant number of pairs who lay two eggs, hatch two chicks, but only raise one of them. Two chicks raised to migration age is the exception rather than the rule, yet the numbers of pairs raising one chick is high. This

cannot be entirely accounted for by predation, and it is interesting, along this line, to follow wild pairs with their broods. The first hatched chick goes off with the male, while the other chick, hatching as it was laid from one to two days later, goes off with the female. While the parents eventually join each other, there does seem to be some attempt to keep the two chicks apart. In the case of an interloping male over the territory, the male parent flies up to escort the transgressor from his bailiwick, while his chick runs over to join the female and her chick. But when the male returns, the chick squirts out to join his father. At night, during the brooding period, both chicks seem to get along fairly well, since they are both lost in the feathers of the mother, and each can hide under a wing. At times, their tiny heads pop up from the feathers like periscopes, to see if anything goes on in the world that they would rather not miss.

In one unusual incident, the male crane had the first chick with him for over a week, due to the failure of the second egg to hatch. Fearing for the health of the female if she sat too long, I waded out to the nest, checked the egg, found it infertile, and reunited the family by taking it with me. It is exceedingly rare to find one egg fertile and the other infertile. In this particular case there was no evidence that the rotten egg had ever been fertilized.

Some recent research with quail eggs indicates that, within limits, eggs set at different times tend to hatch together, the later eggs being stimulated to hatch by the hatching sounds of the earlier. This does not hold true for the Sandhill Crane, however. The hen starts setting when the first egg is laid. The second egg is laid about two days after the first and hatches two days after the first.

It is fairly easy to determine the state of a sandhill family by observation from the air. With two chicks, the parents feed at intervals of up to a hundred yards apart, each having a chick of its own. If both parents are together with young while feeding, it generally means that there is but one chick. If the parents have lost both chicks, there is a desultory, forlorn manner about them, an aimless method of feeding, and their concern at the approach of danger is only for themselves. In sorrow, they fly silently away without trying to protest or to decoy.

In my system of using foster mothers, of course, separation of chicks was impossible unless one used a separate hen for each chick.

Sandy's four young were accepted readily by their bantam foster mothers. The best of the mothers crushed bits of worm in their beaks before offering the tidbits to the chicks, although one pernicious and hateful hen devoured every worm greedily. The baby sandhills nestled well under their hens for warmth and seemed soothed by their quiet clucking.

As the cranes grew, however, the sight became ridiculous, for the young cranes soon towered over the hens and had to squat down to crawl under them. At the slightest interesting sound, the young sandhills would rise up on their long legs, the hens would rise higher and higher, poised momentarily like some strange, long-legged chicken, then the tower would collapse, and hen and crane would end up in an ungainly heap.

Oddly enough when the cranes really outgrew their foster mothers, they would repay their kindness by turning on them quite viciously, and driving the hens away. Height seems definitely a factor here; as long as the hens were taller than the chicks, all was serene. Later on, however, with the situation reversed, the chicks transferred their filial devotion to me. I have always felt that my upright stance somehow fulfilled a basic need and made them accept me as a parent.

When the cranes were big enough to be safe from Horned Owls, they were given their complete freedom. From then on, we did everything in platoon formation. Everywhere I went,

there followed four young cranes, with Sandy in the lead and the Red King grumbling along behind. If I went to the barn, they all went to the barn; if I forgot something and went back to the house, they all traipsed back to the house. This was most unhandy for me if I tried to avoid some grubby detail Gerdi had for me, since she could always tell at a glance which building I was trying to hide in by the cranes ringed watchfully about the outside. We did everything in sevens.

Gradually they lost their downy feathers, began to flap their wings, make short rushes along the ground, and try to fly. At those times, I would stretch my arms and run with them like some strange, flightless, domesticated goose trying to rejoin his wild brethren. At times I would toss a small stick in the air, leap, and flap my arms. Then old Sandy would catch the mood, seize the stick, drop low to the ground, toss the stick as though it was a snake she was trying to dispatch, with a quick flap of her wings, leap high, bow and duck her head with wings half-raised. I would naturally bow, too, and jump high in my turn. Then we all seven would join in a circle, bounce high, duck and run, pirouette, bow, flap, toss the stick, do-si-do, in the fantastic dance of the Sandhill Cranes.

Now, when you're trying on the side to run a tough tradition-bound cow outfit, antics such as this are, oddly enough, suspect on the part of the hands. Like ripples from a stone dropped into a quiet pond, the stories grew around the countryside, and the legend of the strange birdman of Yamsi grew, which in my lifetime I shall not live down.

It was somewhere about here that old Walt appeared in our lives. It was soon apparent as I sat across from him in the employment office that I was in no manner interviewing him for acceptance or rejection. Walt was interviewing me. As I recall, through the mists of a poor memory, the conversation went like this, with Walt taking the opening:

"How many buckeroos you got out on the wagin?"

"Well, er, ah, we don't run a wagon out on the range anymore. We do all our ridin' out of the home ranch and come home at night."

"The ZX, and MC, and any of them *good* outfits still uses wagins."

"Oh," I nodded.

"How many cows you run?"

Exaggerating some, I mustered, "About a thousand."

"Never did work for one of them small outfits. That many cows how come you need a man?"

"My wife sprained her wrist," I said.

"Wife?! You mean there's womenfolk around too?"

"She sprained her wrist on the branding chute"—to indicate that Gerdi was not just *any* woman.

Distaste curled the corners of his mouth in a sneer. "The ZX always had more'n enough good ropin' hands around. Wouldn't have one of them new-fangled chute contraptions."

But jobs must have been a little tough to find that year even for the top hands, for Walt inexplicably decided to come back to Yamsi with me. I tried to slip him as quietly as possible into the bunkhouse, but it was no use. As we drove up, six noisy, clamorous cranes charged up a welcoming storm about the pickup.

"What in hell's them things?" Walt roared.

"Greater Sandhill Cranes!" I shouted back, throwing caution to the winds.

"The hell they are! They look like birds to me. Birds!" Walt snorted. "My Gawd. *Birds!*"

Then began a whole series of incredible events as Walt tried his best to adjust a half-century of habits and standards to our crazy cow ranch. On the first morning, sensing his dislike, the cranes kept him cornered for four hours in the outhouse.

He then climaxed a hard week's riding and gathering by bringing in a bunch of oily steers, only to lose them at the corral gate as the cranes descended on him in a cloud and with great satisfaction thundered the herd away.

He hung his personal laundry out to dry only to have the cranes depart with the odd mates to his socks, one of which still flies atop a hundred-twenty-foot ponderosa pine. And then, for some reason known only to the cranes, they decided that poor Walt needed twenty-four-hour protection, which had the effect of completely unnerving him.

Walt had, at this point, after much urging on my part and a promise I would never let the boys at the ZX know, agreed to milk the cow, a chore the old desert cowboys always thought beneath them. I once sat on the bunkhouse porch with a desert cowboy and watched my nine-months-pregnant wife slip and slide over the ice to milk the cow, and that man never did offer to help her. She made it back with the heavy bucket, too, all on her own. Of course, I'd have helped her, but I'd have lost face, being boss.

I remember Walt grumbling, "What for you milk cows? That stuff ain't fit to drink." Reluctantly he disappeared for the barn with the milk bucket, and I had high hopes; but suddenly there was an outraged roar from the barn, and cranes flew everywhere, shrieking with delight. Walt had milked a good five inches into the bottom of the bucket when one of the cranes grabbed the cow by the tail, and she put both hind feet right in the pail.

As was inevitable, Walt discovered that just after sunrise every morning the boss joined the cranes in a big circle, talked to them as though they were humans, bowed, tossed a stick in the air, and danced with those long-legged birds.

"I thought this here was supposed to be a cow outfit," he grumbled as he headed for the bunkhouse.

The situation grew more and more explosive for some weeks. I lost weight under the emotional impact of Walt's disapproving eye. I began snapping at my wife, roaring at the children, and thinking of trading off my ranch job for some other endeavor, when one morning I chanced to come around the corner of the barn, and there was old Walt himself, hat in hand, gray hair flying. He stood in a circle with the cranes, a big silly grin on his face, and with every flap of his arms, he was jumping higher than I ever had.

CHAPTER

7

By autumn, Sandy's four young cranes, whom we named Eeny, Meeny, Miney, and Moe, stood over five feet tall in their stalking feet, and, with the exception of poor Moe, had achieved near physical perfection. Unhappy Moe! Good luck was not his destiny. Slower than the rest, he invariably came last, whether from weakness of body or mind or a bit of both, I know not. Certainly he tried harder, that bird. Whenever the four flew around the second story of the house to see which room I was in, while we could see three cranes out the west window, Moe would be flying past the window to the east. If the group were dancing, by the time Moe warmed to the dance, the others would have danced out their mood, and poor Moe would have to dance all by himself. Whenever the three would find a nest of grasshoppers, all the luscious morsels would be eaten by the time Moe came bumbling along. But sometimes he surprised me by finding a pocket all his own, and, since none of the others gave him credit for much sense, they never bothered to investigate his excitements. As a result, he got the whole jackpot to himself.

By fall our love affair was in full swing, and the cranes were more devoted to me than ever. The colder the weather, the more they tried to coax me away with them. Perhaps they feared that I would one day fly away to the southland without so much as telling them the way. The instincts for migration were ever abuilding in them, a nervousness, an innate restlessness that made them look often to the leaden skies. They paid less and less attention to Red King and Sandy, their pinioned counterparts, but, full winged and free, they took more and more often to the air, spending long, lazy hours in endless circling, feeding afar in some solitary draw of marsh, but always returning to check my whereabouts.

I could always set them out on an adventure by running along the ground with them, my arms flapping. This would start them in pursuit, imagining that at long last I was about to take off with them. They would be over my head, airborne, and flying afar before they realized that they had left me behind. This was always good for at least a few minutes' peace, for once they felt the sweetness of the air they were understandably reluctant to set wings again for the long glide toward home and would instead soar higher and higher, circling on effortless wings, flapping only occasionally, riding some invisible draft I would never be able to share with them.

And then one morning, when the meadows were brown and sere and the willow leaves along the house spring had turned to gold and sailed off down the stream like so many slender fairy boats, the four young came to take me away. The strange impulse of migration was gnawing hard at them; there was a pathetic urgency in their devotion, as though they realized my limitations and sensed that if I did not migrate with them I should inevitably starve. From the other side of the stream, the old cranes called excitedly. Again and again they came back to me from out the skies above Taylor Butte and Fuego Mountain to the south, came back and called me, pleaded, entreated me to go with them.

However much I wanted them to stay, so little was known of the migratory habits of cranes that I had to let them go, even encourage them. Somewhere along their eventual course, the four tame young cranes were bound to land and cause a sensation, which would give me some indication of the route along which their instincts were directing them.

A cold wind was settling down off the black, foreboding hills, and the leaden sky was sullen with the approach of winter as I went out with them for what was to be the last time. They called excitedly, tugged at my clothes with their beaks, ran, leaped into the air, calling endearments as they flew low over my head. In the distance I heard the King and old Sandy calling noisily. Higher and higher the young cranes rose into the vast skies until they were but light ashes above some far off campfire, a strange mobile of the gods, and then the circles began to slip southward over the ridges and the next valley's glades, and they were gone, caught now irretrievably in the towering vortex of migration, spiraling into the great southern way, flying a compass bearing, halfway between city lights of earth and sky. The valley was lonely without them and empty, and the parents fed, silent and sad, along the frozen edges of the stream.

The snows came quietly then but thick from the heavy, lowering skies, covering my valley with a white shroud. Sandy and the King fought off the cold by wading into the spring to roost for the night. In the early morn, frost made tinkling pie plates of ice around their long, black legs.

Beneath my study, a clear, cold brook rose from the earth, cooing and chuckling as it outgrew its channeled crib, shone through the snowy meadows to become the Williamson, and headed north, then south and westward as the Klamath River to the vast Pacific. Beside the basement brook, eyes glistening like tiny ruby fires in the half-light, the rough-skinned toads circled the furnace or sat out the long winter about the water heater in shrunken overcoats. With each snowbound day a slow but certain step toward spring, we stayed at home and waited, along with the dormant insects, the butterflies in the curtain folds.

At first, after the clamor of waterfowl in the fall, winter seems strangely silent. Then, little by little, as the snow creeps upward on the fence posts, one's ear becomes attuned to the small voices of winter, the Bailey's Chickadee, with distinctive white line above the eye, Red- and White-breasted Nuthatches, the rare and primitive White-headed Woodpecker, the kinglets and the Brown Creepers, all nearly as silent as the snows, their voices scarcely audible above the ticking of frozen sleet on last year's leaf. A flash of blue as a Steller's Jay invades the chicken house in quest of grain—flutterings and cries of anger as I replace the lid on the garbage cans only to find I have trapped a contingent of Canada Jays, who soon forgive me by taking a sourdough biscuit from my hand—a Kingfisher, trouting along the spring, rattles his way upstream to his favorite perch, high above where the spring wells from the mossy rocks—all this I see, and hear, and love. A Great Blue Heron roosts in the jack pines beyond the corral, wild, wary, untamable, a bird of ghastly voice, who seems to enjoy being frightened out of his wits at every sign of life.

Frost coats the whiskers of Babe and Bess, the coal-black Percheron feed team. Flatfoot, our lone Whistling Swan, calls plaintively from the pond as it narrows about him. He is the icebreaker, swimming out the long chill night to keep the ice

back, glad now to associate with the Mallards and Bufflehead who tough out the winter in the gray, ruffled waters of the Upper Williamson.

How often, during that winter, had I looked up at the encroaching hills, at the straight-branched sugar pines along high ridges mingling snow-choked with the western yellow pines, at the bald spots on the ridges where the wind had whirled the snow into mighty drifts, at the traces of what had once been the road to town, looked up and wondered about my four cranes, who had set forth so bravely without their friend, following a trail blazed only by the urges of nature, toward a warmer, unknown land.

Protected by federal laws they were, but these laws protect only if people care. I wondered how many gunners had watched them as they flew by, tame and unsuspecting, hearts filled with a love of humans.

I had notified the Fish and Wildlife Service of their migration and asked to be told of their whereabouts should they become known, but all up and down the western flyway there was silence. I had assumed that, as tame cranes flying over the populated areas of California, they would descend in some farm yard and mooch food on doorsteps, thereby causing enough sensation to deserve a writeup in the local papers, but no such report came to view.

In February great flocks of Western Evening Grosbeaks descended on the cattle feed grounds to work on the droppings for feed or tonic—lovely birds, robin sized, all yellow, black, and white. Then, in the last week, the wild cranes who had nested so long in the Yamsi Valley came home, but still Eeny, Meeny, Miney, and Moe did not come.

In March a farmer in Alturas, California, two hundred miles away, phoned that he had one of my Sandhill Cranes in his shed, so tame that he could walk right up and touch it. Frantically I abandoned the ranch and sped southward. A young girl led me out to the shed and held open the door. Inside, a Great Blue Heron, weak from some avian distress, hissed at me in anger, blinked its great yellow eyes, flopped clumsily with its exertion, and breathed its last. It had been tame, all right, tame because it was dying.

I had no sooner gotten back to the ranch than the Tule Lake Refuge phoned about a crane in one of their fields. This too proved to be a Great Blue Heron. All through the spring, there were more phone calls—and more blue herons. Patiently, I would explain over the phone that herons, sometimes called "cranes," fly with neck folded back, while cranes keep theirs outstretched like a goose; or that herons stand upright, solitary, sticklike, unmoving, waiting for prey, while cranes, often gregarious or paired, walk along, seldom at rest, stabbing at this or that as they move, probing with long beaks half-buried in the soil. Typical was the farmer who called me from Stockton, California. "Hell, I know a Sandhill Crane when I see one!" This too turned out to be a heron, as did all the rest.

These were all good, interested people going out of their way to try to help, and I appreciated it. But popular support can backfire as I had learned as a college student at Berkeley several years before, back in the days when the only four-letter words we had were "hard" and "work." As a student, I had done some work for *Life,* when, halfway through a story I was doing on a tame raccoon for that magazine, the perverse animal got away. The radio and news media were full of my frantic search. The first call came from a woman who had seen one peering through her window watching her as she dressed but I wrote that one off as wishful thinking. There was no chance to check out the leads, for the phones were jangling constantly with hundreds of calls from people who claimed they had seen the raccoon and, I think, were hopeful of having their pictures in *Life.* I had tired of answering the phone when suddenly the raccoons started to arrive in person—or rather *with* persons. A massive coon hunt was now being staged all over the bay area and surrounding hills; the poor bewildered animals were being dragged out of hollow trees, dug out of holes, trapped in garbage cans, captured without regard to personal safety on the assumption that they were gentle. By coincidence, an epidemic of distemper was ravaging the wildlife in the hills, and I was suddenly flooded with all manner of raccoons, some wild and healthy, some mortally ill. At one time I had a room filled with over fifty raccoons dying of distemper and thus gentle, but the one I had lost never showed up. The back alley was filled with torn, bitten, and scratched people, all waiting around to be photographed with what each insisted *had* to be the right raccoon.

After what they had gone through I was lucky to be able to send them home without a riot. Now, years later, an interested and helpful public was finding blue herons instead of cranes.

I was rapidly tiring of the task of chasing down blue herons, when, suddenly, as I was driving along Klamath Lake on my way to Klamath Falls, to investigate another heron, I saw four Sandhill Cranes feeding in a field along the lake. There was something odd about them; never had I seen sandhills feeding in these areas before.

Slamming on my brakes, I careened over to the shoulder, and jumped out. The effect was electric. Behind me, brakes squealed, and traffic backed up as people strained to see if a landslide was starting on the hills above. Out in the muddy field the four cranes probed unaware as I half fell over the barbed-wire fence and rushed toward them.

A man with a face of a mastiff called out, "Hey, Mister! Whatcher gonna dew, put salt on their tails?"

By now, both lanes of U.S. Highway 99 were clogged in a massive bumper-to-bumper jam. No one seemed to know why the first cars had stopped, but, since falling rocks were frequent here, no one seemed inclined to gamble on what someone else might have seen. Since they were stopped, however, everyone was out watching me. The laughter was coarse, derisive.

"Let them make fools of themselves," I chuckled happily. "I'll show them." Mud rose to the knees of my best suit and sucked away one of my shoes.

"That guy must be nuts," a woman said angrily. All up and down the line, people started calling, "Cuckoo! Cuckoo!"

I was untroubled by doubts now. "Just wait," I thought, "until I walk right up to these cranes and they follow me back to the car. I'll show them I'm not crazy!"

"Somebody call the cops," a man said. "That guy needs help."

At that point I tripped on some sort of buried root and fell face down in the mud. Far down the highway, more and more cars were stopping.

The cranes were closer now, eyeing me suspiciously. "Come on, boys," I called. "It's me! Don't you remember your old pal?"

"He's talkin' to them birds," a woman said. "Hey, Mabel, he's talkin' to them herons."

"Cuckoo! Cuckoo!" A hundred voices up and down the line and some of them beginning to be angry.

And then another voice came loud and clear, "Lookie thar, Mama, them birds is flying away!"

And flying away they were without so much as a backward glance. Standing knee deep in black peat muck, I had a good look at them as their long, slow beats bore them skyward, quartering away toward the steep, rocky hillside. They were not my birds at all but two old mated pairs.

The walk back to the car was a long one. No one said a word, just watched, feeling somehow that they'd been cheated. Not daring to look at them in my dejection, I slunk barefooted across the highway, carrying my one remaining shoe, flopped mud and all into my car.

How often during that interminable spring did I stand on the greening meadows at Yamsi, forgetful of my work, watching the skies until the brightness brimmed my eyes with tears. How often did my imagination catch four specks on high; how often did I thrill to wild crane voices high in the faultless blue as the cranes circled north, mere specks, migrating high, headed for some far-off valley not my own. I visited every known crane marsh for miles around, walked out toward the astonished denizens and called, and called, and called. But in the end the cranes always flew away.

Did they really exist? Had some storm born my innocents far out to sea and dropped them exhausted but still trusting upon the angry winter ocean? Had some hunter shot them as they walked toward him for food? Was all this searching of mine wasted time?

In the end, it was. In May, seven months after their migration, I received a sudden clue as to their whereabouts. Lawrence Walkinshaw, author of *The Sandhill Crane,* wrote me from Michigan that he'd noticed a report in *Audubon Field Notes* stating that in December three tame birds, tentatively identified as young Great Blue Herons, had caused a sensation on Bodega Bay, near Santa Rosa, California, some five hundred miles to the south of me. In a statement to the Santa Rosa *Press Democrat,* the local head of the Audubon Society claimed that the blue herons were tame because they were young. Blue herons do not get tame, so the alert Mr. Walkinshaw was immediately suspicious.

The editor of the *Press Democrat* soon tracked down the story for me amongst his December issues and very graciously advertised my plight, requesting information from any of the public who might know of the present whereabouts of the vanished birds.

After an anxious week, I received a letter from a Sergeant Wood. He had befriended three cranes who flew into an air base north of San Francisco and fed them all winter. In the spring, however, they had pulled up all the commanding general's flowers and pecked holes in the window screens, so the general had ordered them summarily dismissed from the base to the keeping of the Fleishacker Zoo in San Francisco. Sergeant Wood had phoned the zoo on my behalf, and the birds were still there. They were now in a roofed aviary with several other species of crane. The zoo, of course, was quite excited at having something the other zoos did not have.

Quickly I wrote a letter to Carey Baldwin, the director, and explained that I had been doing crane research and that these were evidently my hand-raised birds, which we had been using in experiments and which I wanted to pick up.

Back came a letter from Mr. Baldwin informing me that it was necessary to have a Fish and Wildlife Service permit to possess Sandhill Cranes in captivity and that, unless I produced a permit and identified the birds, they would stay in the zoo.

Not to be denied so tersely, I wrote back to say that my crane permit no doubt dated back several years before his and that, while I couldn't identify the birds by any exterior mark, I was sure they could identify me.

Not daring to wait for an answer to my letter, I threw the back seat out of the family sedan, waved to my startled wife, who was about to give birth to our second son and fourth child, John, and started to San Francisco, five hundred miles to the south.

The further I drove, the more my doubts assailed me. I hadn't banded the birds for fear they might hang upon fences if they crawled through. There were three cranes instead of the four that migrated, although I doubted whether Moe could have survived a long, hard journey. Possibly some head scars might remain from childhood attempts to escape the other chicks by fighting their way through the wire, though this too was doubtful. They were obviously hand raised, and mine was the only permit for such work, but then someone might have raised them without a permit. Obviously, the clincher would be whether these birds, fed for some months by a series of strange keepers, would demonstrably be able to recognize a man they hadn't seen for eight months, and then in a far different land and environment.

At the zoo, the officials were obviously startled by my swift appearance and not in the best frame of mind over possible loss of their cranes. I tried to explain that these cranes were of importance to the future of both the Sandhill and the Whooping Crane, but I fear I was, at best, unconvincing.

Carey Baldwin occupied himself with other matters and gave John Malleck, the colorful and knowledgeable keeper of the birds, the task of leading me across the compounds to look.

The cranes were being kept with some Saurus, Demoiselle, and Balearic Cranes in a mixed and varied collection. A crowd of some sixty people thronged the huge covered aviary. My heart skipped a beat as I recognized Eeny, Meeny, and Miney; then, whatever elation I felt turned suddenly to acute embarrassment as the birds wandered dejectedly back and forth without paying any attention to my approach. Miney, I could see, was missing an eye (lost when the aviary lights were turned on at night during

a banquet of zoo officials). The birds fluffed their feathers, Miney first, followed by the others; then all seemed to doze in boredom. A friend I had brought over from Berkeley to witness the joyous reunion grew red with embarrassment for me.

Suddenly I remembered Jan, our young German ranch hand, who had come to us for the summer to learn English. He had always called the cranes in to feed as he milked our Jersey cow. He had gone off to college in the fall, and we soon found that the only way we could get the cow to let down her milk or the cranes to come in for feed was to imitate his accent.

Slipping to the rear of the crowd, I started to call the cows. "Coom Jussey! Coom Jussey!" Inside the aviary, all hell broke loose. Eeny, Meeny, and Miney straightened to full height, called loudly, and stared at the crowd. Then they spotted me. Shrieking wildly, they left the other groups and flung themselves at the wire between us. A short, swarthy man in a knitted cap stared in disbelief. "Say, mister," he said excitedly. "Them birds knows you."

Driving my car to the compound, I opened the rear door, and John Malleck and I pushed the birds in.

It was probably one of the strangest migrations in history. I am a sagebrush-type driver, and the perils of driving through the heart of rush-hour San Francisco with three excited Sandhill

Cranes in the back seat, the action compounded by the howls of a little Irish setter pup I'd just bought, created pandemonium. San Francisco being San Francisco, no one noticed, though the puppy was sticking his head out one slipstream and the cranes the other.

Suddenly, with siren screaming, a policeman shot from nowhere, forcing me to the curb. "Where the hell do you think you're going?" he snarled.

"We're Greater Sandhill Cranes, and it's spring. We're migrating north."

Starved as they were for the sound of my voice, the cranes all hollered loudly.

"Well, everyone else is migrating south. This is a one-way street. You just follow my car. The station is right around the corner."

Well, I tried to follow him, but I'm just not a good enough driver in city traffic. First one car got between us, then another, then I was in the wrong lane to turn, and somehow I never saw him again. Moments later we were somehow on the Bay Bridge, and, fugitives from justice though we were, we elected to save lives by keeping on driving. If they ever extradite me I plan to take the judge driving in traffic, and I'm sure he'll understand.

We had a little trouble going through the toll gate, for every time I would try to hand the gate man a quarter, Miney would try to intercept it. Rather than lose a hand, the man waved us on, but I threw the money into the toll booth anyway and fled.

Everything had begun to smooth out, when a car signaled us off the road, the driver gesticulating wildly. "Hey, Mister," the man called, "you got some birds flew in the back of your car."

I was so relieved to be out of the city, that I stayed there an hour lecturing on Sandhill Cranes, and when we finally headed north again the cranes had another friend.

The further we got from the city, the more the people began to notice and to do double takes. A dozen cars waved us over to ask questions. At length, however, we ran into a different type. As we parked in a drive-in restaurant and waited for food, a stony-faced woman sat in the car next to us and stared straight ahead. For some time she sat stubbornly, refusing to notice the cranes at her elbow. The fact that she could sit next to that gang

and not notice meant that she felt such notice beneath her dignity, and this intrigued me; she must have had her mirror tilted so she could watch. Tilting my head back, I pretended to read the menu and consult with the birds. At the sound of my voice they became excited, tweaked my ear lovingly, and called loudly. I nodded my head as though in complete agreement and once more answered them back. The woman was leaning more and more toward us, straining to hear, when suddenly the door latch gave way and she half tumbled out. Shoving her hat back on her head, she slammed the door, jammed her car into reverse, and shot off, looking, I'm sure, for a quieter place to eat.

As we migrated northward, the cranes became more and more excited, as though they realized that they were headed home to Yamsi and could not wait to get there. Yamsi is screened from the rest of the world by mountains, so there could not have been much chance of them having seen the country through which they now passed, yet the closer they got, the more frantic they became.

Calling loudly, they tweaked my ears until they drew blood, peered out one window and then the other. Every trip back and forth between windows meant crossing the others, wings spread for balance, jockeying for position, croaking angrily at each other.

The last twenty miles seemed interminable, for, although it was hot, to protect my battered ears I had to drive with my hat pushed down over them. Every minute or two, one of them would step on the setter pup, who would feel obliged to complain loudly. At the top of the hill, they all began to dance and flap their wings. Caught up by the excitement, the pup chose this moment to be car sick, and in the ensuing melee I managed somehow to get a mouthful of Sandhill Crane feathers, for all three chose to flop over into the front seat. Through the flap of wing feathers, I managed to get only an occasional look at the road ahead. One lurching crane then caught a toenail in my grey flannels, shredding one pants leg.

Skidding to a stop near the ranch, I pushed open the door. The cranes bounded out, walked a few stiff steps, took to the air, and headed over the trees to the ranch. I arrived just in time to see them drop over the stream and come to a bouncing halt in front of the Red King and Sandy, who were feeding in the meadow near the barn. All three of the youngsters flopped down before the old cranes in greeting, sticking their beaks into the dirt. At long last the prodigals were home.

Moe, the little crane who always came last, was never seen again. It is the first law of nature that only the strong survive. What happened to him is but idle conjecture. Where in that vast expanse does he lie? What killed him—storm, predator, unthinking hunter, poison, or exhaustion? Someone might turn up one day to tell his tale.

CHAPTER

8

Not long after the return of the young cranes, a great crisis swept across my horizons and hung like a black cloud over the whole future of my family and our Sandhill Crane friends. I should be at loss to explain the crisis adequately if I did not first go back into the past.

My uncle, Dayton Ogden Williams, for whom I was named, was the tall, red-haired son of an Episcopal bishop, G. Mott Williams, who, as Bishop of Detroit and head of the Protestant Churches in Europe, was a churchman of note, as well as a brilliant linguist who could preach fluently in six or seven languages. For my uncle, the pain of being one of the bishop's boys was so acute that he ran away from home to prove his manhood in the Peace River country of Canada, where he lived among the Cree Indians. Trapped by heavy snows in the backcountry, forced to live on beaver meat when their food was lost in a snowslide, he and a Cree companion waited out the long winter. Near them, a Cree family, forced into starvation when the husband failed to return from his trap line, had to resort to cannibalism to save the children.

For my uncle, the ordeal brought scurvy and eventual loss of hearing. Just after the turn of the century, Dayton, who had picked up the unecclesiastical name of Buck, drifted into San Francisco with a massive airedale named Pickles and, dog and all, moved into the new St. Francis Hotel, where he and Pickles soon became celebrities. His love for the forests of northern Michigan, where he had spent his boyhood, soon carried him north to southern Oregon, where he began to acquire interests and to help with the pioneering of the lumber industry of the Klamath Indian Reservation.

It was on the northern end of the reservation that Buck first stumbled on the lonely valley of the Upper Williamson. At that time, the valley was a long series of Indian land allotments to which individual Indians had been given title. Through the years, Buck was able to pick up the valley, claim by claim, until he had put together the ranch. This became headquarters and home ranch for his extensive landholdings, the future Bar Y.

My father, Frederick Walter Hyde, a Vermonter, graduated from Yale in 1911, where he was on the football team and led the glee club. He then moved to northern Michigan to superintend a lumber operation for Cleveland Cliffs Iron Company and married Bishop Williams' daughter, Rhoda. Some years later, however, he was stricken with multiple sclerosis, and my brothers and I eventually came west to prep school and the ranch.

I remember, as a green kid, my first night in the Klamath country. My oldest brother, Ted, had preceded me some years before and met me in Klamath Falls, where he outfitted me in boots, Levis, and a Stetson hat, then took me up to Buck's holdings on Klamath Marsh, where they were in the process of branding several thousand head of Bar Y calves. It was the twenty-fifth of June, 1939. Lying in the hay mow of the barn, surrounded by cowboys in their bedrolls, I was too excited to sleep. I listened to the horses, tied in a long row, snuffling and chewing in the hay, listened to the raw night wind creaking the rafters of the old A-frame Grigsby barn. In the morning, I stepped out into four inches of fresh snow.

I had been in the country for some three solid weeks of branding calves and was beginning to think this was all people ever did when I was taken, one evening, to Yamsi, some thirty miles east, over the hills. It was love at first sight. I knew instantly that I had found a place to spend my days, if I could somehow contrive to live there. For Yamsi was nature itself, ducks and cranes breeding in the lonely marshes, trout rising for flies in the placid pools of a summer eve, Wilson's Snipes calling with fluttering wings over the green meadows, Goshawks, loneliest of the lonely, flying swift and low through the thickets, the heady sweetness of blooming clover in the bay meadows, and the cold silence of the mountain winters.

I was always forced to leave Yamsi, but I never again left it in spirit. Septembers, when I went away to Cate School, near Santa Barbara, I would make a moist-eyed ritual of turning my horses out for the last time, and I could not wait for vacation, to see the Mallards in the icy ponds and to find mink and muskrat tracks on the snow-decked logs forming icy promontories over the quiet stream. Behind everything, in my subconscious, was the lonely call of the Sandhill Cranes, so strangely out of my past and yet, had I but dreamed, so prophetic of my future.

Nor could my uncle love it quite as I, for he had come here in his twenties, when the impressions of his lifetime were already formed and his doors closed to anything as deep as I felt; nor would he, who could become tearful on hearing Caruso, admit to an emotional bond to the land.

Above the northern end of the ranch towered Yamsay Mountain, in Klamath Indian tradition the home of the north winds, home of Weaslet, little brother of the marten. Deep into its absorbent pumice breast sank the melting snows, to be born again as the Williamson in a long series of springs on down through the valley. Embracing this valley was a great zone of timbered mountains, a buffer between Yamsi and civilization.

In the course of time, Yamsi became superfluous to the cattle operation, for my uncle was in his seventies and owned more land than he cared to handle. When he went into partnership with my brother Ted, they were more than ever apprehensive as to what might occur at my uncle's death if the organization was not in the best possible shape. In any frank discussion of business between the two, it became more and more evident that Yamsi should be sold.

I was thirty-five years old then. I had left Yamsi many times, to the army in the Second World War, to the University of California at Berkeley. I had been at times a bullfighter, a rodeo clown and saddle-bronc rider, a writer and photographer, and an inventor, yet Yamsi had always called me home. By now I had a wife and four children, all of whom loved Yamsi with a passion rivaling mine, yet I had been working in the cattle business for so long that I had too little money to swing such a deal myself, for Californians were already inflating land values beyond what the income from such lands could justify.

There was also the problem of communication with the old man. He rode us boys hard whenever we failed to measure up. In my case, of course, he had plenty to get concerned about, for I'd made myself pretty much at home at Yamsi, what with my birds and love of nature. I was very careful to ask his permission, of course, for my projects, but it was always when I was sure he had his hearing aid turned off, and then I would do a pretty fair job of mumbling my requests. He would invariably be thinking that I referred to something about the cattle, wave his arms in the air with a "Hell, I don't care what you do!" and depart. Thus armed with such a *carte blanche,* I would build a new aviary for rare pheasants.

Whenever I shouted of the ranch and my wish to buy it (he always seemed to precede such a discussion by turning off his earphone), he would always shout back, "Hell, nobody makes a living in cattle any more."

He was right, and I knew it. But ranching was a way of life for which I was willing to make the sacrifice. I couldn't imagine leaving Yamsi and abandoning my cranes, and I was firmly convinced that no one ever loved the land as I did.

I remember my uncle's phone call. "There's a man named Guber coming to look at the ranch. Got a lot of money; show him around."

While I waited for Mr. Guber to show, I walked back into the pines and found the old tree house I'd had as a boy, climbed up the rusted spikes to the weathered platform where I'd thought out many a childhood problem so long ago. As I lay in complete despair, a tear or two splattered afresh for old time's sake on the weathered, mossy boards. I lay watching the clouds drift by, feeling the groaning deep in the tree's heart as the winds fingered the branches. A Bailey's Chickadee drifted by in a host of merry wanderers and sat for a moment on my boot, while all about the kinglets sang merrily, the nuthatches seemed to do their acrobatics just for me and to fix me with their tiny black eyes from time to time for my applause. I heard a White-eyed Vireo, treetopping me a song, and far off a soul mate of mine, the Hermit Thrush, a mournful sadness, ethereal, almost indistinct, among the solemn north-hillside pines and firs of Taylor Butte.

Ah, how nasty I was to Mr. Guber when he finally arrived and parked his long, shiny car amongst my trees, driving over some young sugar pines I had just planted, while his boys sprang from the car to throw sticks at my geese and cranes. He made test borings with an auger in the virgin meadow, Mr. Guber did, holes that looked even now like the work of a berserk badger. When he asked about the soil, I told him how nothing would grow, and the summer frosts killed the grasses, and the grasshoppers took over and finished off what was left. I told him the winter snows got so deep there weren't any bare trunks left showing from the pine trees, only a few branches sticking bushlike from the snow, how it got thirty-five below for weeks on end, how my uncle was selling because everybody he hired for here died of loneliness and several of the wives had been found hanging in the closet, and how the Indians around were rustling the cattle and killing off the hired men. I told him the septic tank had to be replaced, a forest fire was liable to burn up the ranch at any moment, trash fish had taken over the trout fishing, and eroding pumice from logging operations had so silted up the stream that whatever he had heard of the glories of the fishing in former years was mere lies my uncle had made up to get out from under that awful ranch. And that ghastly soil— if you tore it up to level it, it became sterile, devoid of grass. And diseases! You never heard of such diseases; it was as though we stood on the gates of Hell, afflicted by the vapors. For some reason, when Mr. Guber passed my startled uncle on the hill, he shook his fist at him and shouted something. We never heard from Mr. Guber again.

But there were other Gubers through the years, Gubers after Gubers after Gubers. They all came to me and wanted to know the truth about the ranch—thinking, of course, that I would come up with a bunch of exaggerated lies about how good the ranch was. Instead, I told them all sorts of horrible and obvious tales about how bad it was, and, human nature being what it was, they believed me implicitly. One man even slipped me fifteen dollars for letting him know the truth.

Then came a man who represented a bunch of Las Vegas gamblers who wanted to buy up the valley and make it a pleasure spot, a place where they could fish, shoot ducks, and get away from their wives. He drove up in his big sports car, and when he found out I was the local boy he said, "Say, boy, I'll slip you a ten spot if you'll kind of show me around the valley."

Never in my life having warmed to anyone who called me "boy" or "buddy," I rubbed my hand over my brow in feigned exhaustion and said, "I sure need the money bad but I can't go. Got to spend the rest of my day docterin' sick cattle."

His eyes narrowed to mere slits. "What's wrong with them?" he asked nervously.

"I don't know," I said, "but every other day, I have to go out and give all five hundred of them constipated sons o'guns an enema."

Then there was an endless series of would-be farmer types who took one look at the duck and crane marshes and kept saying how much good a drag line would do, and a big drainage canal right down the center—tear this up and that to be more efficient. I lied, and lied, and lied. My uncle seemed more and more bewildered, but he never appeared to catch on.

In the meantime, the old man could not resist applying the needle about how much money he was going to get from such and such a celebrity to whom price was no object. Each time, of course, as he told it, they would be right on the verge of signing a deal.

Every time I walked the streets of Klamath Falls, my friends would besiege me with rumors. If I pastured some cattle for Claudette Colbert's husband, Joel Pressman, they were going to buy the place. If I ran cattle for Bing Crosby, or he came with Kathryn for a fishing trip, then the whole town stood on its ear. Every rumor made my uncle appreciate more and more what he had and raise the price in his mind as to what the ranch was worth. Doggedly, Gerdi and I raised our family as best we could in all the uncertainty and wondered privately, with anguish, if I didn't owe it to the children to go off and promote the fencing machine I'd invented.

Gerdi being Gerdi, she couldn't help that if she were moved onto the naked desert it would soon bloom for her with flowers, and the worst old shack would soon be spick and span and glow with hominess and pride. I, with her, couldn't stand to see a corral fall down, a gate sag, or a blown shingle left unrepaired, so that often we worked out the long day side by side, making the place glow. For all the lies I told prospective buyers, the fences were straighter, the forests more parklike, the cattle fatter, and the shining meadows brighter and more perplexingly lovely to refute my claims.

And then, one day, old Buck drove up to the front gate, tall, straight, white-haired, hat slouched, in one of his shy, leave-me-alone moods. Without saying a word to anyone, he wandered about, looking at the profuseness of alpines in the rock garden that Gerdi had cheated through the summer frosts, at the new fence about the carefully barbered lawns, at my cranes feeding beside the stream. He wandered through the big stone house, which shone with Gerdi's love, looked at the lovely oriental rugs, fresh fluffed from a morning in the air, glowing in the afternoon light, watched the children galloping bareback on a flashy mare, saw the muddy rivers sweat had made down our cheeks as I and the two eldest, Ginny and Dayton, came in from driving a herd of cows up over the long shoulder of Taylor Butte toward the Sycan and the Teddy Powers meadows. I smiled at him as I trotted up, and my horse snorted and flung himself sideways, but the old man only shrugged and indicated that his earphone was turned off and he had no intention of turning it back on. For a time he stood at the fence in front of the house, lonely, stooped with the years, then he turned and drove off to town and never came back again.

An hour and a half later, we heard the telephone, angry and insistent in the big kitchen. Somewhat bewildered, I heard the voice of Buck's accountant and the words, "Buck wants to know if you want to buy the ranch."

Swiftly, I blurted out the word "Yes," and it was only when I had hung up and was trying to tell Gerdi that I realized I hadn't even bothered to ask the price. But my family and the Sandhill Cranes now had a permanent home.

As I think back through the years, think of the Gubers and all the others, I realize that the old man loved us and really couldn't have sold the ranch to anyone else. He wanted us to have it tough so that we could mature, for he knew that toughness would build character, as it had built character in him. I later learned that for all he grumbled because I was a naturalist as well as a cowman, it was about my Sandhill Cranes that he bragged to his old cronies down on Main Street, Klamath Falls.

CHAPTER

9

The young cranes, Eeny, Meeny, and Miney, soon recovered from their long trip and were once more part of the scene, attendant to my every move to the point of being nuisances. Of the three, Meeny, a female, was the leader and extrovert. Although Eeny was a male, he was plainly second in command, and both of them vied for the chance to boss Miney, who was a lovely, gentle female. But there was about them, as there is about all Sandhill Cranes at their age, a certain reckless irresponsibility, a gay rootlessness, which was possible, of course, since their family impulses were yet more than a year away.

Often they left me now, raucous in their independence, and flew off to some sequestered marsh to feed. I hoped that on these journeys they would somehow find little Moe, but, as they came winging back, sailing leisurely, high above the pines, there were always three and no more. I longed to ask them where they'd spent the day, what lonely marsh had homed them, what soft thermal from what great ridge had held them high, on what lonely forest had their strange, guttural trumpetings of joy fallen. There was *joy* in those flights, no purpose, just the wild, completely irresponsible hell-of-it. I was suddenly like some poor crippled kid down the block somewhere, with three rich friends who all owned airplanes, single seaters of course, who flew all day long, having ever so many adventures, while I had to stay and sell my newspapers to keep my suffering grandmother on morphine. It never occurred to them that someone had to stay home and earn those staggering piles of Purina chow they were putting away every day. I wanted to fly, and sometimes I could spread my wings with them and run and feel damnably close to taking off with them, with the air slipping through my fingers, and gaiety and lightness in my soul, and seemingly so little keeping me from flying. My wife would look at me at these times with troubled eyes, but all she ever said to me was, once, "Be careful you don't go up too high, Icarus. There's a storm coming."

I almost made it once, too. The cranes and I were standing on the hillside by the house and, as we charged down the hill all flapping together and calling our Sandhill Crane happiness call, I found just the nicest sort of little bluff there to go off, and for just a few sweet seconds I was ahead of the flock and traveling fast. This attempt, however, happened to coincide with the arrival of my banker with a carload of Scotsmen from the Portland office, who, up to that moment, had intended to renew my loan. So I couldn't very well go off and leave them.

However inept I was at some things, old Sandy didn't really care. She continued to dog my heels in complete adoration, with the disgruntled Red King, mad and muttering, grumbling reluctantly along behind. She was utterly haughty, utterly imperious, utterly dignified. Every step was measured, premeditated, in keeping with her dignity. ("Opposites attract each other," my wife said.)

From time to time, the Red King would start out on his own, trying to lure her away from me, but the old girl would either ignore him entirely or look back at him with contempt, witheringly superior, as though to say, "Aw go on! You're just a long-legged bird."

If Sandy nested that year, we never found the nest, or it was destroyed before we ever chanced upon it. The following spring, however, a strange happening took place. For some years, Sandy had been at the top of the pecking order about the place, dominating everything—dogs, humans, horses, cattle, and varied fowl—with those lofty and elegant ways. She challenged the airways, squawking angrily at everything that flew her sky, from jet aircraft to the benevolent, circling Red-tailed Hawks. Even when spring filled the air with Violet-green Swallows, she never failed to consider them anything but interlopers in her sky.

As the nesting season began to approach the following spring, she became even more attentive to me and even more in contempt of the huge, ill-tempered Red King. I tried my best to throw them more and more into each other's company, but she considered his species second choice. At times now, the poor exasperated male would sneak up when my back was turned, leap high in the air, and attack me with wing, beak, and slashing toenail to drive me away. But if this valor on the part of her mate in defending his territory and property ever gave her pleasure, Sandy never gave sign.

And then one day, quite unexpectedly, Sandy came creeping to me in abject shame. Gone was the haughty bird I knew. Instead, she was crestfallen and badly mauled, utterly disheveled and pathetically nervous. She crowded against me, squawking miserably, then fled across the fields for the outer pastures, where she stood at last, lonely and sad, as though trying to understand something beyond her comprehension.

My immediate assumption was that some predator had come from the forest. Fearing immediately for the safety of the others, I rushed across the old log bridge that crossed the stream, toward the barn. There was the Red King, standing tall, erect, and regal before a feed trough, and immediately I fathomed what had happened. Close beside him stood Meeny, the young female, in full glory, proud, arrogant, feather perfect, the new queen of the yard. The Red King had finally tired of Sandy's devotion to me and had sought his solace in divorce.

What lovers they were. Standing together near a mineral block, the two cranes were dressing their feathers with red pigment, coloring themselves alike, for all the world like two bobbysoxers wearing matching sweaters.

This coloration process was exciting to me as a crane man. For the first time there dawned upon me the understanding of a

phenomenon I had often observed in the wild, where one pair of cranes takes on a certain color or degree of stain, while another mated pair takes on another. Always before, ornithologists had assumed that this painting was the secondary result of dressing the feathers with muddy beaks. Now, suddenly, I saw it for what it was, an intentional desire to change the color of the feathers, something associated perhaps with the act of pairing and connubial bliss. Or perhaps it was an innate recognition that a color change would make them less conspicuous during the nesting season. Later on I found that cranes were traveling for some distances to use iron-oxide seeps in marshes or other mineral concentrates to dress their feathers. These paint pots would often be surrounded by the footprints of cranes.

This observation now opened fascinating new avenues of thought. If I were to study these wild friends of mine, what better way to mark them as individuals than to furnish the pairs with paint pots of color of my own choosing to replace the natural seeps? Of paramount importance in breeding cranes was the difficulty in getting the cranes to pair and breed. Perhaps by encouraging the pair to paint themselves, they could overcome their reluctance to mate.

Soon the Red King began building a huge, bulky nest along the bank of the spring, dragging in bits of sticks and rushes whenever he could steal them. Since his female was too young to settle down, this was purely a male nest, and she refused to take interest. But they were devoted to each other, and where one went the other was sure to follow. Coloring from the mineral block had proceeded to such a degree that both cranes were now a deep shade of orangey red, while the others remained a light gray. Then too, they had demonstrated another sure sign of pairing: they had started to call antiphonally, with the male starting the call and the female finishing with a short, staccato call so timed as to make the call seem as one.

The Red King appeared to be considerably mellowed now. He seemed content to feed quietly at Meeny's side, a tender and devoted companion to her every mood. Sometimes, as they probed in the moist earth for some unseen morsel, their heads seemed almost to touch.

Poor Sandy! Beaten badly by her own daughter, divorced by the Red King, she sank quickly to the bottom of the peck-ordered heap. Nor were the birds done with her. On the following morning, I picked her up half dead in my arms and carried the wretched misfit to safety.

For months I feared that her scarred mind had suffered permanent damage. She ate sparsely, stayed loose feathered and miserable, or stood knee deep in the stream with head tucked underneath her wing. But, tenderly nursed and isolated, with her gentle daughter Miney for company, she learned, in time, to adjust to the other cranes, living her life on their social periphery, humble where once she was proud.

But sometimes I would see traces of the old queen. When the King wandered near with his young red mate, she would turn her back upon them both, and, with haughty nonchalance, lead her unwed group away. "Four kids," she seemed to say, "Let *her* try that! Besides, I never liked him much anyway."

CHAPTER

10

Old Sandy had hardly gotten over being miffed at our adding a boy, Taylor, to Dayton, Ginny, Marsha, and John, and the resulting case of bassinet neglect she always suffered with a new arrival, when we added a new crane also to the family. She need not have been so jealous of our new cranelet, but she spent a short-tempered week, shouting at everyone and everything about the house lot, before she finally became reconciled and decided that the best way to meet the problem was to ignore it, although it must have been obvious to her from the beginning that this new crane had a special place in my affections.

Even when small, this bird hated confinement of any sort and had a way of getting out of any kind of pen, with the result that the children called him "Loose," which was later changed to a more acceptable form, "Lewis."

Some of the male cranes of my acquaintance have been anything but gentle, but from the beginning Lewis was one of those individuals who "smiled at all he looked on and whose looks went everywhere." He grew to be a big bird, dapper, feather perfect, looking as though he were carved out of smooth, water-worn gray stone. His head was crowned with perfect carmine, and whenever he spoke to me he never spoke with other than a soft tone of endearment.

Lewis was somewhat of a dandy. It bothered him to have a feather out of place, as it would have bothered him to do anything not in keeping with his dignity. He was an emperor, and he seemed to know it. He came from regal stock, a huge pair of sandhills that had lived for years on the Sycan Marsh. Sometimes even the system of the most perfect of birds gets out of kilter, and one year, for some biological reason, his empress mother laid an egg before she had built a nest. It was a field-dropped egg, left to freeze from the cold nights and to rot under the hot sun.

I found the egg in the territory of the giant pair, took it from this orphaned beginning, wiped away the marsh muck and the stains of rotting vegetation, and clutched it to me as though in this great brown blob were all the hopes of future cranedom. New blood for my cranes, a child of superb parents; however inauspicious its beginning, it would be saved. I needed it as it needed me.

Midway in the vast marsh, as I was attempting to cross a slough on my horse, the animal, floundering in the bog, whirled in fright. With its frantic plunging, I lost horse and saddle, then the egg itself. Miserable in the cold black mire, I probed for my treasure, pushed so deeply into the slop that my face went under. A chill spring rain chose that moment to splatter the grime, and an icy wind to rattle last year's rushes. My horse had sought safety without me, and now was dragging reins over the marsh, heading for an island of trees far off across a sea of marsh grasses and tules.

When at last I found the egg, the rain was roaring down violently, and the black water was seething about my waist. The whole marsh seemed to rise. Saturated, the ooze became so thin I had to lie lengthwise to keep myself from sinking into the inky porridge. How easy it would have been at that moment to believe that I, in trying to be kind, had angered the Indian gods of the marsh.

For a time I debated whether or not to hurl the egg off across the swamp, for surely no germ could have survived the exposure and the jostling, but somehow I managed to work myself across the vegetation, trap my errant steed in a cul-de-sac of tules and water, and become horse-borne again in the chill.

Perhaps it was this treatment that tempered Lewis' nature, for in all cranedom there never was one like him. So gentle and kind was he, I should have entrusted him with his great surgeon's beak to pick a hay seed from my eye. I can still hear his gently murmured conversation as we walked together across the fields.

Lewis was a bird of moods. There were times when he liked to be caressed, a most unbirdlike trait, when he loved to have me rub the back of his neck where he was unable to preen. Then he would arch his head against my hand. But then, too, there were times when he found this to be beneath his dignity, and he would move away, never excited, but always with the grandeur of state. Lewis never hurried; in the measured tread of his lifetime, each foot was put carefully into a premeditated niche. Time stood and waited for him, and the world knelt at his feet.

At night he liked to roost at the tip of a grassy promontory, where his reflection, cast by the moon on the silver water of the placid spring, seemed almost to give him regal solace and company in the night. In the morning, he would end our sleep with a shout that echoed far down the lonely valley of the Williamson. It was an emperor blowing his stentorian horn, calling his subjects to awake.

I had great hopes for Lewis to pair with one of my hand-raised handmaidens, to add his regal blood to my tired lines. But one day, as we stood together beside the ranch house, I saw him cock his head, turn his great yellow eye skyward, and then, tipping back his head, call and call to the highest heaven.

In vain I scanned the sky for what he saw. Then, far and faint from the blue a crane answered, and a tiny speck appeared, a female by the call, wings set, dropping on target. It seemed that she had already made up her mind when she called, for she dropped straight from the heavens to his side, and she never left him again as long as he lived.

They had visited only a few moments when the wild princess, seeing me near, called out in alarm, moving straight and stifflegged toward the stream. Already their calling was antiphonal, Lewis calling first and the princess finishing. Then suddenly he seemed to realize what was troubling her, for he ceased calling, walked slowly to my side, and nibbled at my pants cuffs, as though to show that here was not an enemy of cranedom but a friend. She was wary still, but from that moment she began to accept me.

From the beginning it was right for those two. They stood together in the marsh, and, silhouetted by the moon, reflections glowing, they seemed a group of four. Lewis showed her where the best feed was to be found, towed her around, led her to the secret palaces he had along the spring. The two stood for hours in tenderness along the margin, coloring themselves with mud. Pity the incautious male who ventured into his territory unaware, for Lewis the Gentle flew at him with a fury and flayed him with his terrible quick sword, while his queen feigned lack of interest by feeding, unconcerned, along the stream.

Then one morning I saw Lewis alone, but unworried, feeding in the marsh on some rootlet I couldn't see. Perhaps he only shammed, for he was watching me quite obviously as he probed, and I could not see him swallow. When I began to walk among the willows, he suddenly became interested, called once loudly, then tried to insert himself between the willows and me, concerned now at my presence, trying to herd me back with

half-opened wings. I moved back just to humor him, but not before I had spotted the princess, crouched on her bulky nest, beneath the willows bordering the stream.

The female had arrived the first week in May. It had taken almost six weeks of quiet companionship to produce their first eggs. They had built a typical nest of sticks and grasses. Once I knew the location, I discovered to my delight that I could sit at the head of the dining-room table and watch her through the window as she incubated. I saw them change the guard in the evening as she went out to feed, watched her rise from the nest to stand above it for a few moments as she adjusted the grasses and turned the eggs carefully with her bill.

Often I would slip out to photograph her on the nest, but Lewis would always know when I approached and gently but firmly force me away. We were friends still, but there was a new wariness there, a "Look, Buddy, this is my affair. Stay out of it." He could not understand, of course, that I too was proud of all this, as though I had had a hand in it, however slight. Was I not at least an honorary uncle to those precious globes of life? I found myself standing there knee deep in the bog trying to reason with Lewis, but he never gave in, and in the end I retreated, both mosquito- and crane-bitten, to the safety of the yard. Lewis never failed to puff up and growl in satisfaction that he had put me to rout and saved the day for his nest and bride. But, callous female that she was, if she saw these heroics, she didn't appear to notice.

Nor did trickery get me anywhere. I used all manner of devious methods to catch him off guard, but these attempts at sneaking up on the nest when he was off feeding always failed miserably with his swift arrival and served only to convince him that I intended to do the nest some great and lasting harm.

There is not an aviculturist anywhere who does not live for the spring, waiting through the long winter for the first rare egg to be laid at the edge of the retreating snow. Then, when the nesting is a triumph or failure, with the advent of summer, there is again no season for him but spring again, when he has a new chance at correcting mistakes or a new chance at Lady Luck, a chance to try once more.

Had I been able to look ahead, I should have gathered the first clutch and tested them, for I had doubts of the success of so late a mating, since the pairing had not happened in February but in May. After thirty tedious days, my fears proved correct, and the eggs proved infertile.

But I was a birdman, and there was always next year. The pair were more devoted than ever now, calling often in unison, the female in counterpoint, feeding head to head, preening together devotedly. There was time left in their young lives. Gerdi and I sat on the front porch of the ranch house, watching them feed together as the dying sun etched the pine trees black against the golden water of the pond, watched them wade out knee deep into the placid spring for the night. I had such great hopes for them. Red King and his mate had gone to a territory further down the ranch and had gradually drifted away from our headquarters, so, besides Lewis and the princess, there was probably no captive mated pair of Greater Sandhill Cranes in the world. It had taken Lewis three years to mature, and I was depending upon him for my research program. There were so many questions that only close observation of this pair could answer.

"Next year," I told my wife. "Next year for sure." Never had I had a lovelier, more devoted pair. Never had I had more chance of real success.

That summer, the Klamath Falls newspaper sent out a photographer and feature writer to do a story on my work with cranes. I had misgivings that the story would only attract the idly curious, but, since the *Herald and News* was widely read in areas where the cranes needed friends and there was the off chance that the tale might arouse some public sympathy for their cause, I agreed.

Two days after the story was printed, a car drove up the road from town. Lewis and his mate were feeding quietly in a wet spot in one of my meadows. The car stopped, backed up until the driver had a clear view of the feeding cranes through the trees. A shot rang out; Lewis lurched forward lifeless in the ooze.

Reconstructing the scene later from the tracks, I saw where a man had left the car, climbed through the fence, walked to the point where Lewis had fallen, kicked him over with his foot, then walked back to his car. Had I been there to avenge his senseless murder, what jury would have understood?

Merry, gentle Lewis, who so loved to dance, so brimming with life and sparkling good humor. How empty and silent the meadows without his call. And the bereaved—there is nothing more starkly silent and alone or absolute in its dejection than a Sandhill Crane who has lost its mate. God granting, they should have spent the next twenty years together, those two.

Picking Lewis up in my arms, I trudged slowly home, with the princess following puzzled and forlorn at my heels. Every few feet, I would have to stop and show her where the body had gone, for she could not seem to grasp that it was being carried along. Near the house, where the spring flows down through the meadows, there is a small island, profuse with grasses, where, in the summer, grow masses of purple penstemon and yellow monkey flower. There I laid his gaunt gray body, close to where they had had their nest, and left him to his mate. I could not bear to bury him for fear that she would leave.

How faithful she proved to be! For two long years she stayed beside his body, not even bothering to migrate. In time, grasses grew up through his feathers and all but obscured him, but still she stayed. Spring came and passed; a barren spring. No eggs laid; no nest built. If she heard from afar the strident and lonely wooing calls of some single male, she never gave sign, and the other cranes were either immature males too young to interest her or other females, such as old Sandy, and to these she seemed to prefer loneliness.

In time, wild males came in to woo her, but she never seemed to give them much encouragement. One blackguard of a male, whose own mate was incubating in the adjoining territory, began spending his days with her. Perhaps it was her aloofness that first intrigued him. He would leave in the late afternoon to relieve his mate on the nest, but he would return after she had fed, and spend the night standing in the shadows of the pond.

One afternoon the male gave up all pretense of being faithful and deserted his own mate for the sad, desolate widow. Five o'clock came and went. From far off down the valley, I heard her call, saw him stand for a moment listening. Then he resumed his feeding and did not go to her again. His mate raised one chick, but she raised it all alone. The male remained faithful all that long summer, fall, and winter to Lewis' widow, but she never gave him the satisfaction of a glance and died that winter not far from the little island on which Lewis lay.

By spring, the wild male had learned the ropes of the place and was no longer afraid. I found myself dreading the day when spring would come and take him away from me, for he had not found a mate among the other cranes. But one day, to my surprise, when snow still held to the meadows in late February, I heard a sudden goohrah from the heavens, and a wild female began her plane downward. It was the deserted wife. He answered her with a joyous call that must have been full of love, for without a moment's hesitation she joined him beside the stream, accepted his new life with aplomb, and to this day lives with him beside the Yamsi spring.

CHAPTER

11

Sandy never could understand that the neglect she suffered when new babies, birds or animals, entered our lives was only temporary and that, however our time might be taken with other matters, she was really a great part of our daily lives.

Patient as she was, being subjected to the daily tribulations of five children was enough without having to suffer other episodes such as that of the rabbits.

There was a time at Yamsi when it was commonplace, as in Lewis Carroll's *Alice in Wonderland,* to look up and see a large white rabbit scurrying past, and the fact that the rabbit never took out a pocket watch and said, "Dear me. I must be late," only added to the wonderment of the sight rather than detracting from it. It started one Easter, when my daughters, Ginny and Marsha, decided that their pet white rabbit was lonely.

For the girls, with their intimate knowledge of ranch life and the various matings and births about us, the fact that their rabbit, whose name was "Thumper," spent the long spring chasing the chickens around the ranch was ample proof of where the Easter egg myth got started.

When the misguided bunny made advances to a Sandhill Crane some three feet his superior and got a stout peck in the ear for it, we decided it was time these misalliances were checked by finding him a girl of his own species. When we brought her home, they disappeared for a time, and we were just about to explain to the children that a Horned Owl had probably gotten them both when we began to see not just one white rabbit hurrying by but several of them.

Poor deluded fools that we were, we were actually enjoying having them around when the population suddenly exploded. My first awareness of the disaster came on looking out of my bedroom window one July night to see the ground was white with snow. I woke Gerdi when I discovered that the snow was moving. The ground was covered with white rabbits of all sizes and shapes. As I flashed a spotlight around, the reflection of their eyes made up a whole city of lights. My wife only yawned, shrugged, and went back to bed. "In the morning we'll have an Easter egg hunt," she said.

Sandy, of course, was beside herself with the intruders and kept a dozen or more cornered beneath an outhouse. Our few old Horned Owls, unable to cope, grew so fat and lazy that they had to blink both eyes at once to keep their balance. The fact that many of the rabbits spent most of their time under the huge stacks of alfalfa hay, where they had unlimited feed and lots of time to raise families, made the task of population control almost impossible. To all outward appearances, the stacks of hay remained quite normal, but as I stepped on one of them I suddenly fell, like Alice, into a long hole. The whole inside of the stack was a maze of rabbit warrens.

While I was toying with the genetic approach of introducing a lethal recessive, my wife had the practical answer. "You'd better learn to like rabbit stew," she said.

Eventually we began to catch the rabbits by running them down. If guests drove up, we interested them in a new game we were playing, and soon rabbits were being exported by the automobileful. We ate rabbits boiled, fried, fricasseed, baked, stewed, sauteed, casseroled, and in salads. The poor

Horned Owls, who only ate them raw, were now using their wings to prop themselves up in the branches, and once they dropped on a rabbit they had to pick a low branch to climb back up the trees.

At last we began to get ahead of production, only to find that various rabbits were being held out on us by the children, to protect the species. They were suddenly mocking me with my own words, using my Sandhill Crane findings to protect their rabbits from extinction.

Every rabbit seemed to have a name based on its home. Whenever I tried to catch one now, it was, "But that's Bunkhouse Harry, Daddy!" or "That's Outhouse Fanny!"

"Just two rabbits?" Marsha pleaded, blond hair flying.

"Just one male rabbit!"

"Your father is against motherhood," my wife said, but Sandy, at least, agreed with me.

Still burning with this last unfair accusation, as I was riding out on the ranges looking for signs of cattle rustling, I found two dead porcupines lying along the side of the road where someone had killed them only moments before to collect the bounty. Dismounting, I took my pocket knife, and within moments I had delivered from each, by caesarian section, a tiny baby porcupine. These I laid gingerly across the hairy breasts of the mothers and slapped them into life. To me the miracle was not that they awoke but that the mother porcupines had been able to put up with them as long as they had, for the baby quills, even before hardening in the air, were sharper than those of the mother. I have a theory, now, that this may explain why porcupines in the woods cry and wail a good deal. I leave the actual research to someone else, but I have it all figured out that the ones we hear crying are the pregnant females.

I also have the theory that when female porcupines nurse their young they hold very still, for at the slightest motion, the nearsighted little porcupines, minutes old, would whirl and slap their tails at the movement.

I suddenly discovered that I was now able to answer a favorite question of my daughter. "Yes, Virginia, porcupines do get quills in their noses." As one little porcupine went tumbling up to the other, the second one whirled protectively and slapped him

across the nose with its tail, leaving that one black bare spot a forest of tiny quills like the rest. Ten minutes after delivery, I was pulling quills out of a porcupine's nose. This may explain why I never seem to find more than one baby to the mother.

Careful not to rub the little ones the wrong way, I soon had them dried off. They had sparkling little black eyes, and silky black hair, which extended beyond the white quills, making them appear quite innocent. When I made a quick motion, however, the quills stood on end, and wham went the little tails right at their benefactor. If I sat quietly and chuckled to them, however, they would climb right up my shirt front and try to nurse on my buttons.

Soon, I won their confidence, and was able to pick them up by sliding my hand under them gently. Of course there was now the problem of mounting a cranky and neurotic horse, already unnerved by the strange smells. I crowded the animal's head into a tree and flung myself aboard. The porcupines had no chance to learn riding slowly, for once I hit the saddle I was hurtling the long miles toward home at a gallop, with a porkie in each hand and the reins held loosely in my teeth.

Sandy, still feeling neglected, was aghast at the addition of porcupines and turned her back and marched stubbornly off to the fields, where she fed out on the marshes for several days until her pique was over. One of the wonders of family life, however, was that my stock as a father, at such low ebb after the disaster of the rabbits, could rise so rapidly with my children when I came home with baby porcupines. I was no longer the cruel tyrant who had ordered the summary execution of my children's rabbits.

One baby porcupine, weaker than the other, did not survive. It was given a procession, hymns, burial, and sermon by a ten-year-old minister (Ginny), then was tearfully interred in the vegetable garden, joining a host of family pets, including snakes, frogs, butterflies, Cedar Waxwings, hawks, owls, dogs, ducks, geese, salamanders, and Sandhill Cranes.

The other baby responded to feedings of milk from an eye dropper to become a devoted friend to the children. It would shuffle along behind them on endless trips about the yard, so slow in its journey that it never got more than halfway somewhere before it met the children coming back. If one of the children sat for a rare moment in repose, the little shuffling black pincushion waddled up with great delight, climbed up clothing until it reached its favorite perch on a shoulder, then pacified itself by nibbling an ear lobe.

Despite stern orders from me as commander-in-chief that the beast was never to set foot in the ranch house under peril of immediate death by violence, it soon became common to meet it at night shuffling down the hallway as one groped one's way barefooted for the bathroom. It took up a permanent lair under my chair in the dining room, perching on the rungs beneath, leaving a host of puddles and shed quills. We all got the permanent habit of checking out a chair quite carefully before sitting down, a habit that, being with me still, is hard to explain to a waiter at a city hotel who is holding one's chair.

Along with its diet of milk, it soon began eating greens, clover, willow bark, corn, dog food, apples, and other fruit. A good part of this was stolen from the pantry when no one was looking. It loved, however, to be discovered and herded about with a broom, whirling about and sparring with its tiny tail of sharp, detachable quills.

Answering to the name Pork Chop, it enjoyed being picked up and carried, but this had to be accomplished slowly and carefully by slipping one's hand under its soft underbelly. I seemed to be pulling quills out of me most of the time, but the children were limited to one or two a day. Often it would climb halfway up my person, then slip and bounce all the way to the ground, leaving a puff of quills wherever it touched. Sharp to the extreme, they had to be removed immediately, since they had a way of working through clothing and suddenly imbedding themselves in my flesh.

When the children called, it would come snuffling and chuckling from a tree or around a corner of the house, where it had been eating my wife's flowers, and would tag along its bumbling way as long as anyone was patient enough to wait for it.

It always greeted any approaching motion as danger, turning its tail, and raising its quills; then, satisfied in its nearsighted little world that a friend approached, it turned to stand on its hind legs to get a better look. Sniffing the air with its tiny black nose working, its quills would lower, and it would shuffle up to beg for a handout.

Porcupines are highly destructive to forests, since they seek out the tender cambium layer of bark, thus girdling the trees. To reduce their numbers, a bounty had been placed on them. Bounty notwithstanding, Ginny and Marsha were soon befriending them in quantity. Cages appeared everywhere with all sizes of porcupines. In a weak moment, I brought in an odd white one I found. Every time I would find one on the ranch and get out of the car to destroy it, Ginny would leap in front of it and say, "Not that one, Dad! That's Prickles," or, "That's Joey."

My wife's garden was soon a shambles, her rose bushes eaten to the root, and the front pasture grazed to the soil. Thus nourished, Pork Chop had gone from a matter of ounces to some thirty pounds. When time came for school in September, Pork Chop got a pleasant new home in Klamath Falls at the park, where he was the delight of children and keeper alike.

"No more pets!" I shouted at the children, while Sandy tipped back her head and agreed with me in the loud language of the Sandhill Crane. The kids merely looked at one another and smiled, and I had to think back to the Yamsi of an earlier time, when I had a score of falcons, eagles, and owls tethered to the front fence, as well as a good working friendship with half the denizens of the forest. I was a lonely boy, and they were my solace, as they have come to be my children's through the very example I set for them.

CHAPTER

12

Sometimes I see my children eyeing me quizzically, wondering, I suppose, how their strange father got that way. So many road forks taken, and never any chosen with the clear sense that it was logical or right. So much in one's life left to chance. Perhaps the die was cast many years ago for Sandy and me when first, as a lonely child in the northern Michigan woods, I turned to nature as a companion.

From that time on, the influences have come from a wide variety of strange sources. A boy named Aubrey Swinton drowned in a canoe in Lake Superior, and his mother, knowing my bent, gave me his cherished bird books. I remember sitting for long, happy hours with my gentle father, who had been struck down with M.S., watching a Chipping Sparrow bring up a brood in the young cedar tree beside his screen porch. And once I found this big man, who had played football for Yale and had been a lumberman, crawling on his hands and knees through the rocks to save the lives of the young nestlings when they were attacked by a snake. Somewhere in my files I have a kind letter from Fred. C. Lincoln, the late head of the Fish and Wildlife Service, advising me that I had been turned down in my application for a bird-banding permit because of my age. I was nine.

And then, without much premeditation on my part, there was the West, Yamsi, and horses, Cate School (a boy's school near Santa Barbara), and the headmaster, Curtis Cate. For all his brusque ways, he saw the inevitability of my leanings, sent me on trips with the Santa Barbara Museum of Natural History to the coastal islands, took me to visit the naturalist Donald Culross Peattie and to see films such as the photographic study of the California Condor and its fight for survival. Somehow he left me with the realization that there are no limits to our endeavors save those we place upon ourselves.

Into that confused welter of forming ideas that is the young man in his late teens came another influence, and that, oddly enough, was the poet Alfred Noyes. I was astounded to find that my feelings for nature and my philosophy had evolved independently in someone else, and in a person of some acclaim. It was a timely little push, and I needed it badly.

I was a senior at Cate School then, during one of the early years of the Second World War. I saw a new boy, who had come of late from England, lonelier perhaps than I had ever been, sitting quietly by the hour watching a gopher dig his hole. I too was a gopher watcher, and I felt the impulse at that moment to go to him and tell him about my tree perch hidden amongst the Yamsi pines. His name was Hugh Noyes, son of the famous English poet we schoolboys came to know and love. His father, Alfred, had brought his small family here from England, while he taught and lectured in our universities. We came to know him as a friend. In the evenings, while rain and fog drifted from the channel islands, and the far-off lights of Santa Barbara hung war-shrouded in the gloom, we boys retired some fifty strong to the comfort of a commons room, where Alfred Noyes stood before a glowing hearth, balding, portly, troubled by glaucoma, and poured out his soul.

When he recited "In Sherwood, in Sherwood, about the break of day," or "Come down to Kew in lilac time," how that great, husky voice roared or trembled soft. To us boys the virility of manhood lay suddenly not in our baseball gloves, folded like closed-winged bats in our athletic lockers, but in the smell of lilacs and the awesome mysteries of nature herself. From the dust of our anthologies, his poetry came suddenly, vividly to life. From the lips of the man from whose soul those songs were first sung, we felt the nearness of the thing and trembled.

And Mary Noyes, how many times had she followed her husband through those ringing lines? Her face, worried somewhat with the years, shone at those moments with so great an affection that she was truly beautiful.

The daintiness of her! She came often with her husband to tea at Eric Parson's house. Eric was a sun-browned, shaggy Chips of a master we boys all loved. He taught me English, and I wrote reams of purple prose for him, which he loved and my classmates justifiably hated to the man. For Mr. Eric, I wrote of quiet rivers and the shy ethereal music of the Oven Bird, and he was off to his boyhood in Maine, or to England and Robert Browning. For long moments we were free to the wandering thoughts of boyhood, while he carried on. For this, with the usual disrespect of schoolboys we called him Foggy Eric, but we loved him more. In one's lifetime good teachers stand as islands in the mists. A Miss O'Conner taught me grammar; Foggy Eric put purple in my prose.

What magic there was in those quiet, California afternoons at tea time at Eric's house, in the company of the Noyes family. I watched the faint, blue-veined trembling of her hand as Mary Noyes poured me tea, hardly daring to look up at the warmth and twinkle of her eyes. Through the soft haze on the blooming ceanothus, I found for her the quiet monotony of the pallid Wrentit, the faint rustlings of towhees and thrashers, caught for her the wing flash of the Phainopepla and the bustle of the Bewick's Wren, while Alfred Noyes listened bemused or homed on England with his quiet voice.

> For Noah hardly knew a bird of any kind that isn't heard
> At Kew, at Kew in lilac time (and oh, so near to
> London)*

---

*"The Barrel Organ" by Alfred Noyes. Reprinted by permission of Hugh Noyes.

At graduation time, as we eight seniors, starched rigid in our blue suits and white shirts with detachable stiff collars, sat awed and proud that the long arduous road through Cate was finally over, Alfred Noyes stood before us and sent us out into the world. Miracle of miracles, it was as though he spoke especially to me, so closely did he mirror what was in my mind. As I heard him, he talked of God and the order behind the universe, of the pattern of the leaf, the composed, ordered brilliance behind a bird's song, veins of an insect wing, design of a butterfly. For however we doubt, however our advancing knowledge shreds belief long held, it is the order, the composition by an unseen hand that we cannot explain, that must, in the end, when all earthly secrets are discovered, remain to mystify us and to let us believe in something.

* * *

In the woods east of the stone house at Yamsi lies a forest of lodgepole and ponderosa pine, made thicker by the impudence of the young trees, which have somehow managed to start up in competition with the old. If one looks closely here, one can find the debris of a decaying tree and, amongst the refuse, a few old rotten boards, all that remains of what was once a tree house. Built in the top of a great lodgepole pine, it was my retreat during the storms of childhood, a place where I spent long dreaming hours visiting my undemanding friends, the birds.

It was at best a precarious perch, built with a child's love of driving nails, which even when they did not split the brittle boards purloined from an old cement form seldom made contact with anything that made the perch structurally safe. Of the hundred or so nails, there couldn't have been more than four or five that really mattered or contributed. But somehow the edifice clung there through the storms of many a winter, piled high with snow, and outlasted my childhood, though not my need.

It was my delight to climb there, to lie hidden, in the midst of a fragrant pine forest with only a few lacelike branches between me and an intensely blue sky, a boat in the green sea, gently rocking, and my body feeling the rhythm of the winds floating at peace. Somehow the tail of a Red-tailed Hawk, circling high on the thermals, glowed transparent against the sun, each separate pinion feather on the wings feathering alone, isolated from one another by a jagged canyon of silver sky,

High above, the Sandhill Cranes circled, their faint goohrahing floating down from afar, as through the mists of time. I hear them now, and I will hear them long after they are gone, in the stillness that is their future. Endlessly circling, ashes from a sage fire, gray and transient, caught in the gentle vortex of a wind, higher and higher, now just this side of the dim banks I once thought were the edge of Heaven.

As I lay there looking up into the vastness of the sky, God looked down, a strangely gentle, strangely saddened face, hair and beard fleecy like a cloud and, often as I stretched up my arms to Him, He only smiled. No body, only face and hair and beard, like the Mount Rushmore Lincoln. If his voice came to me in the soft lyric soughings of the winds, I never understood, nor could I quite fathom the faint call of the circling cranes, like trumpets from the distant land.

As I looked up at the branches silhouetted here, the order behind nature came to me, the composition and rhythm of it all, molecule to molecule, not just jumbled together but planned by a higher hand than ours, the lacework of the needles, leaf patterns, frost, fern, and mould, silvery music of Hermit Thrush, shy, wistful, ethereal, like some far-off waterfall. No, not jumbled, but composed—first the delicate pure silver of the note and then the music, by the great unknown composer. Call him God, if the name really matters. Wind in a pine forest, counterpoint of warm summer rain, yank of nuthatch, laughter of swifts, thunder of angry summer storms: not the voice of God, perhaps, but echoes from His heaven.

I used to project myself in those treetops, forget my identity, my troubles, and be for a time the Bald Eagle, soaring, exploring the rugged white cliffs of the clouds above the black-firred forests of Taylor Butte, or the Sandhill Crane calling to defend its territory. I was the happy and sociable Violet-green Swallow, a bird of constant laughter; the Mallard male, raucous in nuptial flight; or Wilson's Snipe, wing-singing through a long, warm summer eve. Bright-eyed weasel, little brother of the marten; mule deer doe of mincing tread; chuckling, bumbling porcupine; or pine squirrel, guardian of the wood.

To project oneself, to be, to feel, and to understand, to sense a kinship, an identity, this was the delight. What sights I saw from there—the swift-winged Goshawk, fiercest of the fierce, loneliest of the lonely, skimming headlong through the tress but a few feet above the ground, inches from disaster. For the ground squirrel, life was but chance, a case not of "if" but of "how long" before it happened to scamper across the swift bee-line shadow the Goshawk drew across the forest floor. I watched the Horned Owl, Clark's Nutcracker, Canada Jay, all nesting in the cold, young almost grown before spring, and after a storm I found pine needles scattered like myriad brown wishbones in the snow.

Sometimes in the winter woods came a silence so intense one could hear wood borers in a rotten log, many feet away, digesting their way, bite by bite, through the toughness of the wood, or the tick of sleet against bark or withered leaf. Then soft, as from another valley, the feathered upside-downers, all competing for the same tiny mite in the same tiny crevice, a cloud of mixed varieties moving in harmonious discord through the forest, each ignoring the others, yet managing not to be left behind when the crowd moved on. Chickadees, Brown Creepers, Red- and White-breasted Nuthatches, kinglets, tiny voiced all, but insistent, leaderless, defying gravity to cling and feed on the bottom side of a branch. A tiny bill seizes some invisible delicacy, and it is gone into the tiny furnace; one instant's energy, no more, and the endless search goes on through the waking hours. The pines are alive one moment with the flutter of their wings; then they are gone, and the forest is even more silent and lonely without them.

In the spring at nesting, what sights I saw. How many families did I spy on from my perch. I saw the Cowbird lay her egg in a White-eyed Vireo's nest, watched the tiny parents struggle to feed the voracious foster child, saw the young vireos kicked from the nest, cheated of their home by the usurping guest. I heard the raucous young Cowbird chase the vireos through the pine tops, insistent for more food; then, justice of all justice, I saw a least weasel, no bigger round than my forefinger, dart from a crack in a dead snag, seize the upstart Cowbird, and drag it into the heart of the log, away from the worried flutterings of the foster parents.

At the rear of the old log blacksmith shop, I could just see an old canteen, hanging in the perpetual shadows, the home of many a brood of Chickadees. How frantic the spring search for holes by Mountain and Western Bluebirds, Hairy Woodpeckers, Flickers, the gaudy, rose-breasted, crowlike Lewis' Woodpeckers, White-headed Woodpeckers, Violet-green Swallows, nuthatches, and creepers. Juncoes were common nesters in the duff of fallen logs, as were White-crowned Sparrows, whose song I welcomed. Red-winged Blackbirds along the willows, gaudy Western Tanagers, vivid in yellow, orange, and black, Steller's Jays, intensely blue. Mallards and Cinnamon Teal in the grasses of the meadow at the edge of the forest; Wilson's Snipe and Sandhill Cranes along the quiet borders of the house spring.

Short-tailed and golden-mantled ground squirrels, chipmunks, brush rabbits, pine squirrels, foxes, coyotes, deer, Bald and Golden Eagles, buzzards, redtails, Sparrow Hawks, Evening Grosbeaks, Kingfishers, Barn and Cliff Swallows, Western Flycatchers, warblers—Audubon, Yellow, Pileated, McGillvray's—crossbills, Purple Finches, siskins, all these I spied on from my perch. If they knew, they never seemed to care. Often as I lay, a pine squirrel bounded across my foot. A Chipping Sparrow with rusty cap tried to steal the laces of my boot for its nest, and from then on I kept a country store there of horsehair, feathers, and string.

No one ever followed me to my hideout. Had I died there of some sudden, swift attack, no one would have known to look for me there so close to Heaven, and those few crazy, twisted boards were lost in the crazy, twisted limbs of the lodgepole pine.

Margaret Biddle, my uncle's aunt, would come out on the back porch to call me to some task I hated, girl's work mostly, inside the house, and I would lie there on my perch, smugly silent, enjoying the way her jaw clenched in irritation when the forest greeted her in silence and I did not answer.

Even in her seventies she was a terror, that woman, and the disharmony of our relationship drove me more and more to seek denizens of the forest for company. The young expect too much of adults, and when I could overlook her failings I came to appreciate her more.

I suppose that up to the time I became exposed to Margaret Biddle, grownups were either all good or all bad. What an enigma this woman was for me, for she was good and bad without being a blend. The qualities remained separate in her, making her diverse. If I am a second generation in Yamsi's history since Indian times, Margaret Biddle was the first, and loving Yamsi as I did I came to appreciate her as such and to be more tolerant.

For what I was witnessing was the great era of Yamsi. Buck had taken Margaret Biddle in as a partner in the Yamsay Land and Cattle Company, and she lived in the big stone house and gave it an air it will never have again. Even the buckaroos ate on silver plates on the long oak table. She was a lovely woman, and cultured, but half cat.

We had a different cook every week, for the old lady just couldn't resist being nasty. The eggs were too hot or too cold; the meat had too much salt or not enough; any oddity of speech or dialect she picked up and mimicked cruelly. One big cook grabbed a knife, backed her into a corner, and told her to keep the hell out of the kitchen, but the old lady ignored her. There wasn't a bit of fear in her.

What a horsewoman she was! No bigger than a minute, she'd crowd some half-outlaw up to a stump and sweep aboard. Four reins and an English saddle on a cranky old spade-bit horse. Yet the horses loved her and did anything she asked.

However frosty the morn, she made the cattle drives, even at seventy, tough as whang leather but, have no doubt about it, a lady. When the buckaroos were all sagging in the saddle, twisting one way and then the other, trying to get comfortable after a long day, she was still straight, still elegant, still in command. I see her still, eyes blue, complexion cream, alert and active, yet she could out-cuss half the buckaroos on the ranch, when something crossed her. She brought the drawing rooms of some gay foreign capital to the barn with her, and the men were her slaves and remembered her with gifts and cards long after they had moved on. I suppose the cooks never forgot her either.

With the departure of every cook, Buck would cuss her out the way he would cuss out a man, threaten her, rant and roar at her, until the tears would come to her blue eyes, and trickle down the wrinkled ivory of her faultless skin. She'd capitulate a moment and promise him to be good. Just one more chance. But each new cook wouldn't be in the kitchen at Yamsi five minutes when the old lady would breeze in, gracious as all get out, getting in the way just when the cook was trying to hurry a meal for a dozen men, making her do things over in ways that made no sense. The men would stare down at their places in embarrassment as the poor cook would be cut to pieces trying to serve the meal. A few days, a week at most, and it was all over. The cook's Irish would be up, and she couldn't get back to town fast enough. Perhaps some of them would have actually killed her had they ever been able to find in the woman some sign of fear, some flaw in the perfect steel. Always for a few days then we were left with her cooking, and the old lady could just barely boil water to make tea.

But hostess she was, and it didn't matter how obscure or how famous the guest, she treated them with equal charm and gave Yamsi an elegance that made slaves of all of us. She was the queen of France, but born in a new land a century too late.

She hated me at times, and had it not been for my tree house I couldn't have taken it. My brother John came once to Yamsi for a Christmas holiday from Cate School, and the old lady made him do housework until he was ready to drop. Then, just when she might have come to accept him, she left him reading on the floor with a kerosene lamp that had to be adjusted every few minutes or it smoked. When she returned, he was still sprawled on the floor deep in his book. The whole house was lined with black soot, and the only clean spot was the place on the oriental rug where John had been lying. John couldn't wait for vacation to be over and settled in the east, where he could be sure never to see her again.

Then suddenly I saw the good in her, a spoiled aristocrat perhaps, used to lots of servants and attention, but filled with culture and as good a horsewoman as the West ever produced. Whenever she had her difficult spells and handed me a mop or a dust rag, I would interrupt her to talk about the Western Tanagers I'd seen or the meadow gentian I'd found, and her eyes would sparkle with interest. She'd call me a dear boy, then, and forget for a time to have me do the household chores.

She always wanted a tame cat, but she never got one. Once in a while she would bribe a cowboy to capture one of the wild barn cats, and these she would attempt to tame by locking them up in the house. You had to be careful opening a door for the cats couldn't stand to be in the same house with her and would hit all the walls trying to get away. The first door opened in the morning had a cat charging through it, and then she was mad all day.

She owned a series of wire-haired terriers, which always barked, always chased cars, and were always run over out on the road. Cars very seldom came that way, but when they did they would cost the old lady a dog. At one low point of our long relationship, she lost a spoiled, useless terrier named Johnny. I buried the dog for her under a pine tree at the corner of the yard. I thought I played taps for the dog on trombone, though years later I found that the taps I knew was actually reveille.

But she cried on my shoulder anyway and thought I was the nicest boy ever after that. From then on we were good pals, each easing a little of the other's loneliness. I remember her driving me to the station that fall to go back to school. She had on a little bonnet that was always slipping down over her eyes, and she was so tiny she could hardly see over the dashboard. I glanced at the speedometer, and we were doing ninety on a gravel road, while she sounded me out in a Victorian way to see if I knew about the bees and the flowers. I had the temptation to tell the old lady I did, in no uncertain terms, but I was afraid she'd run off the road.

After her last visit to Yamsi, I drove her down to Santa Barbara. She happened to be collecting Green Stamps at the time and had a credit card for some off-beat oil company she owned stock in, with the result that whenever we got low on gas, we couldn't find the proper make of station with the right kind of stamps, and we were constantly running out of gas. I was often tempted to hand her the gas can and send her hoofing it, but I never had my uncle's courage.

Not being used to traveling with old ladies, I kept ignoring her more and more urgent requests for me to stop at a service station so she could brush her teeth. I was in a hurry to make Santa Barbara, where Gerdi waited for me, and kept thinking that since her breath seemed all right I might as well put up with it as long as I could. After several hundred miles of this I looked over to see the lady in great pain.

"Young man," she stormed, "I'll have you know when a lady my age wants to brush her teeth, she damned well means something else!"

In restaurants she was impossible, sending back her food to the kitchen time and again. Near Stockton I took her to a special place I knew for dinner to cheer her up. The place was elegant and busy, and we had a cocktail while we waited for our number to be called for a table. The storm broke when she thought the headwaiter had let someone in ahead of us. Sailing up to the bewildered man like the grandest of grand duchesses, she accosted him in no uncertain terms and strode out of the place, while I slunk meekly after. Never in my life had fresh air felt so good. We had just gotten into the car when she turned to me and said, "My goodness, I've left my nice new gloves behind. Be a good boy and run back in and get them for me."

It was her last trip to the ranch, and I never saw her again, but she is often in my thoughts, for she had a great effect upon Yamsi, and by driving me to seek solace in nature she had a great effect upon me.

CHAPTER

13

Perhaps at no other time of the year is the stone house at Yamsi quite so gloomy and filled with foreboding as in March, when the north winds sweep up the valley and drive away all hopes for an early spring. Frost grips the daytime puddles along the half-open roads, so that the huge Percheron feed teams slip and slide and clatter as they feel out a foothold, then strain against the tugs to start a load of hay out to the cattle.

But in the midst of the gloom there is the excitement of new arrivals, the cranes coming in from the south, the Canada Geese taking up territories, and Sandy's own ecstatic welcome of newcomers from a vantage point on the front porch. She seems to welcome, not only the faint, far-off voices in the sky when first they drift over the southern ridges, but also the smallest warbler voice new sung from the surrounding willows. For her, the long winter is over regardless of the weather, and once more things will be happening to excite her.

At Yamsi, this is the time of calving, and every day new little calf faces show up on the feed grounds, as, tottering out of the sheltering pines and windfalls, they join their solicitous mothers in the feeding herd. More than likely, the calves congregate in a nursery group of their own, often supervised by a baby-sitting matron but often alone, as the mothers lick up the hay scattered for them over the frozen meadows.

Now and again, an impatient baby calf wanders out through the cows, looking for a mother in the five hundred strong and getting gently kicked away with every error as the learning process goes on. Now and again a heavy cow, belly distended with hay and calf, flicks her tail nervously as the birth process begins, then wanders off, feigning nonchalance, seeking the shelter of the pines, where she finds a windfall, screened from the wind and prying eyes. From beneath her tail, a sack forms and distends like some giant, blue star sapphire, and, as she lies and strains, the sack breaks, flooding the pine needles with pearly fluid. Soon come the yellow and white front feet of a tiny calf, then as she strains and rests and strains again, the first pink of

the nose, then head, then strain on strain, shoulders, gaunt ribs, flanks stained yellow with body wastes, then hips, and, at last the calf comes with a final rush, breaking the cord.

For a moment the cow's eyes glaze as if in relief; then instinct begins to play, as the first odor of the newborn calf reaches her heaving nostrils. Bawling low, she lurches unsteadily to her feet, turns, and with great rough tongue licks the afterbirth away from its quivering nostrils, pushing it with her nose, confused by a feeling half between love and anger, until the calf's faltering breath comes with a gasp, the tiny sides quake, and the heart pumps hard with the first shock of the cold. Instinct has taught the mother to clean up the mess of birth, and when the calf is licked clean she soon chews up its former home, the great, pink, buttoned flag of afterbirth. Then for a time she lies quietly down beside her new charge, as her body rests from her ordeal.

But the coming night is chill, and soon, when she has ceased her trembling, she rises slowly, licks the calf and nudges it, until its surging instincts make it struggle up on its stiltlike legs. Time and again it falls, and each spill sends the blood racing through its veins. New strength comes, and with it balance. It chews away at the cow's brisket as though trying to devour her, then, slowly, the cow noses it back along her flank. A dozen times it falls to rise again, then suddenly, its chewing lips find the long teat, its tiny tail wags back and forth with the rhythm of its sucking, as the first colostrum milk, yellow with magic, warms its body, distending it with hot life.

From the dusky shadows of approaching night, a coyote sniffs cautiously the smells of birth, then goes its way amousing across the still frozen meadows. It has learned better than to bother a cow with her new calf. As the night frost settles, tiny beads of ice form along the ridge pole of the calf's back, but inside the new milk has the radiant heater going, and the young one nestles to the side of its mother in contentment.

There will come a time, a day or two hence, when the cow will hear the muffled tread of giant, dinner-plate Percheron hooves, the rattle of chains, and the squeak and rumble of the feed wagon. She will leave the calf for a time to feed, but soon she returns. Little by little, she lures it out of the forest of trees into the forest of cows, where its dim vision at first confuses it, until it learns its mother's special voice and smell from the others.

Another calf butts heads with it, slips on the ice, and runs away. When the sound of sucking makes it think of food, it invites itself to dinner, only to be kicked sharply away by an alert mother not its own. Then soon, from the bewildering forest of legs, its own dam calls to it and nuzzles it contentedly as it begins to suck.

It is a cow's world, and my world, but it is also Sandy's world. She wanders at will amongst the feeding cattle, and if a curious cow sniffs at her, Sandy defends herself with an imperious thrust of her swordlike beak, and the cow settles back contentedly to her hay. Sometimes she flies up aboard the wagon and pecks at the fallen grain upon the floor, but mostly she walks, for her high center of gravity makes it difficult for her to follow the lurch of the wagon.

The Percherons know the way, and, from the time the heavy harness is thrown upon their backs, hames buckled about the padded collars, belly band hooked, pole strap linked to quarter straps, and tails lifted over the britching, they are in the routine of the day. Ponderously, one steps over the wagon tongue and stands in place, working the cold steel of the bit, while the other sidles to the tongue. Reins are thrown over the backs, neck yokes and tongues hung clanking from the collar chains, tugs fastened to the singletree, and the empty wagon, creaking with the frost, bounces over the frozen ground as the team pulls it to the haystack.

Load after load comes from the haystacks to the fields. Each morning, the team gives the stack an appraising glance as though they know that when they have hauled out all that hay spring will have come, the grasses will be a sweet, juicy change from winter hay, and they will be turned out to foal or simply to laze until next winter's work.

For the teamster, there is something of a feeling of power as his wishes flow down the long ribbons of leather reins and the massive beasts strain obediently against the load. He stands, feet wide, braced against the reins, knees slightly bent against the jolt of the wagon. There is perfection here as the great hindquarters before him sway in step, the eveners straighten, noses line up into a photo-finish tie, ears prick forward attending the road. A murmured word and the horses ease their ton apiece into the work. Stop, go, wait while the man opens the gate before their noses, then move the wagon through, gently now, without hooking its corner against the gate. No driver now, but the horses, knowing the routine, pull through the gate and stop, waiting for the sounds of the man closing the gate and climbing back on the load.

Midway in the morning, the horses pull past the silence of the hay trucks, oil thick with cold, wheels useless in the snow. The team passes with disdainful glance; in this modern age we use trucks for the long summer hauls, but in the winter only the teams are able to start in the thirty-below weather, able to wade the drifts when hundreds of bovine lives hang in the balance, waiting for hay the horses are sure to bring.

One man, a team of horses, and seven hundred cattle are fed on time. The juices start like clockwork in a cow's stomach, and the hay is there. Today, tomorrow, seven days a week, until the green grass comes and the cows, relishing the change, refuse the hay.

High on the ponderosa ridges, snow drifts silently on snow, a quarter of a hundred miles of trackless forest between us and civilization. The world could be dead a week, and no one at Yamsi would know. From the outer world, in winter and early spring, come only the winds, needing no road.

From time to time, Al Shadley, our old foreman of Indian descent, wearing in this modern age a Stetson instead of the headdress, Levis instead of buckskins, glances at the ridges, from the gentle, protective shoulders of Calimus Butte in the south to the balding thrust of Yamsay Mountain to the north. He watches how the snow of the last storm clings to the trees, how the pine squirrels keep to their nests, how the steller's Jays and the nutcrackers are noisy or silent, and he knows the weather to come.

The teams are Al's pride. Every hair of the manes is roached with loving care; the horses lean against him as he stands upon the empty wagon after work and bow their necks forward to be clipped. Sometimes they waken from their day dreams with a start, then stretch their necks meekly again as the shears sing

against the coarse, heavy mane, and their gentle eyes glaze. He takes no Sunday off the winter long for fear someone else will drive his teams. And, when he touches the lines, ten thousand mysterious volts pass down them, making the horses bow their necks with pride, and pull, and pull, until the wagon comes or something breaks.

In the long evening he sits and listens to the wind murmuring about the eaves and the tick of the stove adding heat to heat. Already it is ninety plus and the stove a cherry red. It is a modern stove, thermostatically controlled to smoke a log through the night and keep the house a gentle, even temperature, but after five years and many a lecture of mine he has not accepted this. He finds a pitch log, dripping with amber, which blacksmiths used to weld with long before acetylene, and he is happier with a new pitch log than with a new automobile. The stove for a time outroars the wind; my old setter slinks away to find a cool corner two rooms away, where a slight breeze comes up the damp, secret world of a mouseway. Hotter and hotter the room becomes, warming the old man's bones, and the silvery thatch of his hair spreads drowsily over the crest of the sagging armchair.

How well we know each deer he has killed, how he outwitted each horned monarch and fired each shot. How many great bucks in his sixty-odd years? The tug chains clank anew as he drives each memory team; what runaways he has in that old armchair. We feel the dust of cattle drives long past, thirst, and the bite of alkali on Oregon's vast sage desert. We hear the spling of kindling splitting as he cut wood for historic Tobey Riddle, the Winema of the Modoc Wars. "She was an old woman, then, short, fat, and thick, and she bought wood from my father and hired me to split it."

In the wise old humor of his voice flows the spirit of the Klamath country, for he came here as a boy from the Pit River country in northern California, when history had just started. There was the witch, White Cindy, man or woman he never could decide. Old tales of scaling timber, the Indian agency, the one-room school at Yainaix, bug camp, forest fires, Huckleberry Mountain, jerky, Klamaths, Modocs, Paiutes. Childers, Ida and Lee Coburn, Mamie Farnsworth, Coyote Moore, Bill Bray, gone all of them, and yet you feel that somewhere there in history they pause to wait for him.

One tale he does not tell: falling from the wagon one winter's day, a broken back, alone and no help for thirty miles, six hundred hungry cattle bawling in the snow, all day long crawling on hands and knees, he brought them bales of hay until all were fed and his team unharnessed in the barn. Only then would he crawl home. There will be no more like him when he is gone.

If he is full of tales of latter days, he has the old ones too, the legends of the Klamaths about the little people of the forest. Whenever one makes a statement in which he does not believe, the silence can be monumental and more eloquent than words.

I remember the time Sandy had followed me up on the haystack, and I was sitting on a bale of hay watching her probe for mice. I studied the steaming breath of the team drifting ghostlike away in the chill air and sat there musing, while the old cowboy smoked a cigarette. I failed to notice a large meadow mouse that crept out of the bale beside me, driven by Sandy's long bill.

Suddenly there was a whir of feathers, and a tiny owl, not much bigger than the mouse, shot past me, missing my face by inches. There was a shrill squeak, the mouse was dead, and the tiny owl sat clutching his prey with needle talons. Its tiny head bobbed up and down challenging me for possession, yet not quite knowing what part of me to look at. He was the size of an English Sparrow, with fierce, snapping, yellow eyes, brown striped breast, and brown back spotted with white. Snapping his beak as Sandy tried to take the mouse away, this little buzz saw of an owl whirled off suddenly into the pines, hurtling the mouse away with him.

"Those little owls are bad luck," the old man warned.

He must have read the derision on my face, for the silence came then. The next time I heard the Pigmy Owl piping from the timber, I imitated the whistle, The piping came suddenly closer now, soft, ventriloquial; in vain I tried to find the little owl in the treetops.

"Bad luck," old Al muttered, and I laughed outright, teasing him as I often did. But I remembered that the little bird had been a bad omen among the local tribes. A chill went through me, but I had gone too far to back down. As I teased the little bird with my whistle, there was a sudden whir of wings, and the tiny owl landed on a branch some inches from my head. I was silent now, for my lips were dry, and I feared that at this close range the little owl would detect a flaw in my mimicry. Eyes bright, the little pigmy bobbed up and down, trying to find the other owl. Then with a blur of wings, rising and falling as it flew, it disappeared into the forest.

Amused by my new plaything, as we drove down the meadow, I whistled again, and almost immediately from the tree above us came the answer. The little owl was following us, his piping voice regular and monotonous. "He's putting a curse on us," I grinned, slightly tired of the game already. That was when the wheel fell off the wagon, dumping our load of hay in the snow.

The old man was silent as we fixed the wagon and fought the hungry cattle away from the spilled bales. Once we were loaded, I leaped to the wagon, seized the reins, and started the team. As they strained against the load, there was a sudden crack like a rifle shot as a tug broke and a singletree slewed sideways. There was nothing to do but drag each bale out over the snow and feed the hay right on the spot. It was tough work, and the owl never missed a beat.

Suddenly, as we fed, there seemed more cattle than usual, and as I finally looked up from my work the grim truth struck me. Somewhere a gate had come open, and a hundred bred heifers we had been keeping separate were suddenly mixed with the cows.

Tomorrow was another day, but as soon as I came out of the house the owl began his piping. The old man's face was dark, his jaw set; Sandy seemed nervous and irritable. I did nothing to encourage the owl, but still he stayed. Gerdi, Dayton, Ginny, Marsha, John, and little Taylor helped us separate the heifers, while the owl sat up in a tree and never seemed to miss a beat. Poe's raven and not bigger than a minute.

At the end of a long chute we were using to doctor a sick heifer is an iron maiden of a cattle squeeze, which catches the cattle by the head and holds them tight. Somehow, the catch slipped as the animal hurtled through, and the long arm of the gate caught the old man in the ribs, sailing him into the snowbank twenty feet away.

"What's that funny piping noise?" my wife said, looking up into the tree.

"It's a bird of ill omen," I said.

"Maybe it's an omen pigeon," she suggested, helping the furious old cowboy out of the snowdrift.

That afternoon I saddled my horse and rode out the front gate, through the snowy forest. Whistling, I called the owl to me. With a buzz of wings it showed itself ready to follow. For several miles, I led the bird away, up the mountain and down the far side of the ridge toward the drainage of the Sycan. This was good hunting country; everywhere were tracks of mice in the snow. I was silent now as the tiny owl piped for me. Stealthily, I rode away; the tiny voice seemed even further and further in my past.

Chuckling to myself, I rode on into the ranch. "He's gone," I said to everyone. "I took him clear out of the valley to a spot where there are plenty of mice for him to eat." The old Indian gave me a dark glance as he sat looking up into a scraggly Jack pine. There on the lowest branch sat the little owl.

By the next day there were two sick calves—no symptoms I could put my finger on, but they were definitely off feed. While Al listened, I tried my best to get the idea across to the veterinarian over our country line. "Maybe it's that doggone Pigmy Owl," I ventured, shouting.

"Ten cc's of penicillin and a warm enema," the vet shouted back.

Tired of shouting, I gave the prescription to old Al, and he limped out of the house, nursing his ribs.

The next day, as we loaded the wagon, the little owl piped from the tree above. "You win," I told the old cowboy. "I'm sorry I teased the owl." Dropping from the stack, I moved some oat bales, and found a nest of little mice. Even Sandy got into the act and helped me capture them. As fast as we dropped them on a bale, the little buzz saw would take them away, without even a glance of thanks.

For the rest of the day, all was serene, and every day after we made a point of offering him a fat mouse or two, delivered on an altar of hay. The calves, of course, seemed suddenly to flourish.

That spring, nature stepped in, and the owl went off to seek a mate in some far-off valley's glades. We never saw it again, but to this day, when I whistle at my work, I'm careful of the tune.

A few days after the owl's departure I asked Al about his sore ribs. He said, "You know, with that ten cc's of penicillin and that warm enema, I'm feeling pretty good again."

CHAPTER

14

Sandy's lifetime at Yamsi is but a decade and a half, and mine but a third of a century of the valley's total history. Compared to more settled areas, of course, Yamsi's known history is quite short and quickly told.

The early Indians summering in the valley of the Upper Williamson were probably desert Indians. Points found beneath the pumice superstrata are similar to those found on the desert near Fort Rock. On the surface of the pumice one finds the lesser points of the Klamath tribe, Indians who came to Yamsi to fish, to hunt, and to gather the seeds of the yellow water lily, which was called "wocus" and was pounded into a meal.

With the eruption of Mount Mazama, some six thousand years ago, much of the country east of what is now Crater Lake National Park was covered with a thick mantle of volcanic pumice, hundreds of feet thick in places. Although the rainfall of this desert area east of the Cascades was only twelve to fourteen inches, the pumice sand stored a great percentage of this, and soon the land was covered with vast forests of lodgepole and ponderosa pine, scattered with springs of cold, crystal-clear water.

Since Indian times, the ranch has had only a slight touch, really, of civilization. My uncle took over from the Indians, and since he was a bachelor my family is the first to grow up there. For this valley, history has really only started, and its history is more Indian than white. There is a challenge here, fields that only a decade ago were desert areas of white pumice are now lush, bluegrass pastures, heady with the smell of clover. Often the new idea of today is the improvement of tomorrow. Progress is measured by the distance rash youth plunges ahead and does not quite return to the experienced methods of the generation past.

The accent is on water. At the headwaters of the Williamson, not far from the ranch house, the water bubbles joyously forth from the lava bowels of the pumiced earth, but from here on the stream is serene and quiet, as though prolonging every moment of its stay in my valley. Here and there, throughout its course, more cold, sweet springs flow from the hillsides, so as one proceeds north through the ranch the stately Williamson becomes less a stream and more a river. On the sandy bottom, there is a constant drift of pumice; here and there, tiny snowstorms of sand constantly rise and fall with the bubbling of a bottom spring; sandbars erode slowly with time and are gone.

North, at Wickiup Spring, ten thousand gallons a minute boil from great fissures in the lava, doubling the size of the stream. In the midst of the river, a heavy boil marks a shaft, blue and deep, where lurk large trout in the bone-numbing chill. They are but fleeting shadows in the mysterious gloom of this nether world and never bite the hook. In the shallows of the spring, round green sacks of colonial algae, called "mare's eggs," live out their unexciting lives, unaware that they are found only two or three other places in the world. Cut loose somehow from the stream bottom, they drift on northward with the slow pulse of the silent water.

This is not rattlesnake country. Legend has it that long ago the Indians made a deal with the rattlesnakes that if they would stay south of the Sprague River the Indians would never harm them. To this day, the rattlesnakes have upheld this treaty. The Sprague seems, however, to be the dividing line between the

Mazama pumice deposit and the original clay, for seldom does the pumice extend south of the river. It may well be that the abrasive qualities of the pumice irritate the snakes' skins and allow parasites to enter, thus limiting the reptiles' territory.

It is easy to understand the attraction this lovely valley had for the summering Indians. Even in the early 1900s, when my uncle first arrived, waterfowl darkened the sky, and spawning trout were so thick it appeared that one could walk on their backs. Indian families still camped here in numbers, smoking venison, waterfowl, and fish over willow fires. Trout of fifteen pounds were common; my uncle often scooped up the evening meal of fish in a dishpan; pelicans gorged so heavily they could not fly.

These lovely white birds once circled the Klamath country in graceful formations numbering in the thousands. One aged Indian told me of a place he found, high on a ridge overlooking Klamath Lake, where the old pelicans went to die, where the ground was littered with hundreds of dead birds, some only skeletons. Today the number of white pelicans has dwindled sadly, and soon perhaps they will be gone for all time. Their dominance of the Klamath scene can still be found in local names—the Pelican Cafe, the old White Pelican Hotel, Pelican City, Pelican Bay Lumber Company, Pelican Butte, or in Klamath Union High School's athletic team, the Klamath Pelicans.

The Indians were a busy, active people, primarily concerned with the business of gathering food. Lithe young Indian children lay by the dozens along the banks of the river, tickling trout by stroking their bellies, until their deft fingers were locked in the gills. I once watched an Indian boy build a simple snare of wire and move it carefully through the water over the head of a monstrous trout. The fish never moved until a swift, flashing jerk sent it flying over the boy's head. Primitive, but how devastatingly effective. Nets were used too, centuries back in time, for we have found several grooved stones undoubtedly used as net weights. Women waded the chill waters by the hundreds, driving fish into the nets.

Wickiup Springs was a favorite bathing spot. The Indians heated stones in small huts along the shore, poured on water to make steam. Then when they were steam cleaned, they dashed out naked and plunged into the thirty-eight-degree water.

While the smoke from willow fires somewhat bothered the flies, they still ganged up on the drying meat. I remember a rack of drying jerky old Cindy Crume had on her ranch on the reservation near Sprague River. There were so many flies it was impossible to see the meat, but somehow the jerky dried before the eggs hatched, and to the Indians protein was protein.

In 1910 the wet meadows along the stream at Yamsi were a sea of willows, so thick that it was nearly impossible to fly fish unless one waded out into the stream. Probably the extensive seas of willows accounted for the fact that some four hundred Ruffed Grouse haunted the long meadow, known since Childers' time as the Bull Pasture. Childers, who lived for a time at the head of the valley, told me that there were also a few Prairie Chickens here as late as 1915. With so much cover, the birds were able to resist the Horned Owls, which, I feel, later had a great part in decimating the population. Now there is only an occasional Blue Grouse on the high hills to represent the species.

As late as 1940 broken remnants of dugout canoes could be found along Klamath Marsh and the upper river. That year I was fording the river on horseback when I spotted a perfect canoe on the river bottom. Taking my riata, I built a loop and pulled the canoe to the surface. It was neatly made, appearing for the moment to have hundreds of nails driven into it, but these proved to be the larva cases of the caddis worms. I removed my riata, determined to come back later, but I was never again able to find the old canoe. Released of its overburden, it apparently moved downstream with the current and in some lonely backwater or another was once more covered with the shifting sands.

Traces of the old Indians turn up at odd times. During a recent flood, a rancher was watching the swirling Williamson near its mouth when he noticed coming around the bend an Indian paddling a dugout canoe. As the object swept on past, the Indian turned out to be a bush growing in one end of the hollow log. The canoe was swept on out into Klamath Lake and to my knowledge has never been seen again.

I used to fish in an old dugout in the Williamson. Fish were bigger then, before logging of the forests eroded the pumice hills and choked the river with sand. A little Indian boy and I used to fish the pond at the headwaters together in this delicate craft, in sort of an uneasy truce with the river gods. If we wiggled, we tipped over and had to swim ashore in the murderously cold water. We were good for no more than one big fish an evening. When a ten- or twelve-pounder struck, we simply fell overboard and fought the fish ashore.

Even in this present generation, life centers around the river. My uncle wandered it in his lifetime, using a tiny silver spoon with a long cane pole, casting only once or twice in each pool. His fishing expeditions often carried him twenty miles down stream. But I and my children are fly fishers, working each riffle and cut bank, wasting none of the stream.

For us the river is a world to be examined minutely—the insects hatching; birds feeding; ducks towing a raft of downy young ones; deer slipping out of the dry forest, open mouthed in thirst; beaver, inquisitive yet shy, floating only with eyes, nose, and ears showing, quick to dive with a thunderous slap of tail if we dare so much as to breathe; muskrats moving up and down the currents, bound for some favorite beanery of succulence.

So common are the muskrats passing by that we have made a fine art of casting for them on light tackle, snagging them beneath the chin and landing them. Fishing once with my sister Liza's husband, who arrived at the ranch from Vermont, I snagged a huge muskrat and landed him after a stirring, ten-minute battle. Holding the four-pound beast by the tail, I called to the Vermonter in triumph. He glanced at the muskrat casually. "Pretty good," he admitted. "What fly you catch him on?"

Not five minutes later, one of his sons, not to be outdone, snagged a seventy-pound beaver. Pole, line, tackle, and boy sailed into the river.

This upper river is a dreaming river. To know it at its best is to drift down it of an evening in a canoe, letting the slow pulse of the current carry one through fairyland. Drifting through the marshes, one moves through another world. Tall cattails rival the pines as an immediate horizon to one's world. There is a distinct, jungle-like quality to the sounds; they are wild, varied, often so intense as to be almost overpowering. Hundreds of Yellow-headed, Red-winged, and Brewer's Blackbirds croak and shriek from the rushes. Yellowthroats cling to sloping perches of grass. Western Marsh Wrens rattle back and forth on nest-building binges. These sociable little wrens number in the hundreds, each building several extra nests without doors, as though to decoy from the real one. A thousand acrobatic Nighthawks cruise the stream, with long white-banded wings, in open-mouthed pursuit of insects. Myriad Violet-green Swallows nest in the dead trees near shore, dashing helterskelter for insects above the water. Kingfishers rattle up and down from one favorite perch to another. Black Terns in ministerial garb, graceful forked-tailed Forster's Terns, both noisy as fish wives, work the surface for minnows or tiny insects. Wilson's Snipe dive from the heights, blue herons squawking as they flush from the bends, drown out the chitterings of that swept-wing racer, the Vaux's Swift. A Sandhill Crane calls assurances to his mate on her nest.

In the bends of the stream, the trout are fat and lazy. Eastern brook trout are pigs that know no end to dining and grow so fat and deep they seem ready to burst. Often in June hatches of a forked-tail called the black drake blacken the water and turn the trees along the bank into slippery masses of wings. Even when in the pools there seems to be no open water, still the brook trout rise to gorge themselves.

But the rainbow exceeds the brook trout in size and is a moody feeder. There are times when the river seems sterile of fish, devoid of all life. Then, quite suddenly, with their mood, as summer frogs are wont to sing or cease, a flyhatch starts, a caddis nymph rises to the surface and flies away, then another and another. Suddenly the rainbows begin to rise from the deep, gently at first, then faster and faster until several are in the air at once. These are the times when a snarled line can drive a fly fisher to madness.

Sometimes on moonlit nights big rainbows like submarines seek out the shallows to feed and play. Great backs show in the moonlight; silvery ripples play up and down; waves lap the shore. A few short minutes and they are gone whence they have come. At times like this the fisher hardly dares breathe. Excited, he or she casts badly, catches a tree, remains hopelessly inept until the last big fish has ceased its wanderings to move back to its world of half-darkness in the blue depths of some quiet spring.

There comes a time, in the evening, when suddenly the great chorus of frogs ceases its song. A cold shroud settles along the bottom lands of the river; insects, sensing the chill, cease to hatch and the trout to rise. A bat flits along the stream, black against the path the moon makes upon the cold water. Far off up the hillside, a Horned Owl hoots, and the whole valley is silent in sleep.

This is the time when fires are lit even in summer in the great stone fireplace at Yamsi, and fishers and cowboys recount their tales. Here in the course of a week the whole history of the valley is recounted by one teller or another in a host of tales. Those who have lived and worked here are not many, but each seems to have left some little part behind, some little immortality, forgotten by the world but living again and again at the Yamsi hearth, as Yamsi history—for history is, in a great sense, people.

With the progression of people at Yamsi has come a metamorphosis of a wet valley into a developed, working cattle ranch, a prodigious effort, done in the main by hard work and sweat. Yet people are remembered not so much for their works as for those idiosyncrasies that made them differ from one another.

Fifty years ago there was old Scotty, who kept a tame badger in the bunkhouse; there was Ern Paddock, my uncle's first foreman, who used to pack an endless supply of water from the spring so that his wife, Etta, could wash the crew's clothes. There was Al Farnsworth, who was always falling asleep on mowing machines, who, on divorcing his Indian wife, Mamie, sold Buck the lovely Wickiup Springs area to spite her. Homer Smith, a gnomelike foreman with a bull voice, great nose, and more personality and spirit than a dozen other men, never managed to go to town without causing a brawl and ending up in jail. Ash Morrow, who always managed to get lost, rode our tough old bucking horse Whingding to a standstill in front of the ranch house, when the curb strap of his bridle broke. There was old Walt, who danced with the cranes, and old Charlie Tucker, elephant man in circuses, cavalry man in China, who couldn't walk past the most gentle rooster without being attacked. I sent Charlie once to mend a drift fence up on Yamsay Mountain, but he wandered into a Blue Grouse's hooting territory, and the bird, with sacs distended, ran him clear down the hill. There was

Frank, with high crowned hat and handlebar moustache, who drifted into the country leading three ancient horses, the youngest of which was being ridden by his dog. Frank compounded a legend of ferocity about this ridiculously friendly tail wagger, whom he kept to guard his possessions, and we never had the heart to spoil things for him. Ever mindful of his personal dignity, whenever a guest would come along we would say, "Watch out for Frank's dog. He's a dangerous killer." The old man never failed to look pleased and mysterious and proceed to embroider upon the tale.

In the passage of time, the cranes too are fast becoming part of history. The young Sandy grows through middle age into an old dowager. Every year we raise a succession of new cranes, some of which merge with others into a blur and are faintly remembered, while others stand as individuals, such as the Red King, Lewis, or the princess, never to be forgotten. They are part and parcel of the daily life of the ranch, part of the scene. It is hard to remember that their way is a difficult one, that there might not always be cranes at Yamsi, that those great marsh voices might one day be stilled for all time.

CHAPTER
15

After sexual maturity is reached, birds do not go on changing as do humans. Sandy for instance seemed the same bird at ten as she was at five, the same at fifteen as she was at ten.

The ranch, of course, in any five-year period, showed the scars of human energies—new ditches and canals, new land under irrigation, new fences and corrals. The rough old bunch of Hereford cows Gerdi and I started with have, through selection and purchase of outstanding bulls, grown into a large, uniform herd. Our five children, bursting with the health and independence of an outdoor ranch life, grew rapidly into active forces about the ranch.

But the progress I was most concerned with, developing knowledge and understanding that would one day save the Sandhill Crane from extinction, went on slowly. Some years there were no real gains at all; in others, the gains were quite dramatic. Whatever the year, I went on raising Sandhill Cranes, trying to fathom the birds and understand their needs, so that we might help them meet the challenges of the changing world and survive the furious onslaught of civilization.

The gray Greater Sandhill Crane, and in no less sense its rarer white cousin, the Whooping Crane, is a highly specialized bird. The more highly specialized a wild thing is to its environmental needs, the harder it is for the species to adjust to change. Everywhere civilization encroaches with a rush upon the sandhill's territory. Change is everywhere, even in the once lonely West; adjustment is imperative if the species is to survive.

For the sandhill, food is not a limiting factor, for the bird is quite varied in its diet, feeding on grains, insects, rootlets, bulbs, small rodents, frogs, grasshoppers, dragonflies, weed seeds, tadpoles, fresh-water shrimp, in short, just about anything edible a marsh or meadow can produce. Marsh is needed only for nesting, while much of the actual feeding is done on diverse sites. I have observed them, for instance, in sagebrush flats, miles from water, feeding quite happily on whatever this desert terrain could supply. Even such an arid environment can be varied in its supply of food, producing small swifts, spiders, rootlets of such edible desert plants as the apau, as well as seeds from grasses.

Aside from small damage done in pulling up newly planted grain, the Greater Sandhill Crane's diet is most beneficial to the farmer. I watched a single pair of cranes destroy a grasshopper nesting of some four acres. The pair camped on the spot for several days, tearing up the nests, eating what young hoppers they could digest, shredding the rest upon the ground with ever-active bills. This nesting could have spread over hundreds of acres, but when we arrived to survey for the possible use of insecticides, which are costly and dangerous, there was no longer any need. The sandhills had done the work for us.

When Oregon recently had one of the two greatest outbreaks of meadow mice, or voles, in human history, Yamsi escaped serious damage, because sandhills, hawks, owls, badgers, herons, and coyotes were present in sufficient numbers to stem completely the advancing black tide. The cranes did not devour all that they killed, but one stab of that probing beak, a shake and toss, and the vole was dead beside its burrow. They enjoyed no greater delicacy, however, than the small nests of pink mice, stolen from hideaways amidst the clumps of grass.

At the time of the vole explosion, I had a pair of tame cranes about the fifteen-acre house lot. Voles were beginning to riddle the ditchbanks with their tunnels, and to spoil the meadow. In the house lot, however, the tunnels ended abruptly, just a few feet inside the fence. Often as not, a fat black vole was left lying dead, a punctuation mark at the end of his run. Having a balance of nature that year saved us from suffering damage that could well have run into thousands of dollars.

Much of the probing a crane does with its beak is in wet lands, where such aeration is of benefit to the soil. Then too, the sandhill is skilled in the removal of nematodes and other agricultural pests. If they sometimes become a little over-enthusiastic in my rye fields, I have learned to shrug it off and scatter a little more seed especially for them, knowing that I will end up with more of a crop at harvest time, in the long run, because of them.

If the sandhills fail in their struggle for survival, then, it will be not because of lack of food but because they have failed, in production, to maintain their numbers. Nesting habits are one great limiting factor. The large, long-legged birds, visible for miles across the marshes, need a suitable niche in which to nest, a special wet, tule-marsh habitat. In spring such suitable

environment helps stimulate the reproductive organs. Eventual success or failure of the species will depend in large measure on its ability to accept other types of breeding environment, such as meadow or sagebrush. This adjustment alone would give them many thousands of acres of additional breeding area.

A bird of loneliness, the sandhill will have to become more tolerant of the presence of human beings, for loneliness, even in the West, is a thing of the past. Often nests are deserted simply because they have been visited by a well-meaning ornithologist or a curious farm boy. One pair I knew were bothered by some grazing steers, which, shipped in from California, had never seen a crane and followed the sandhills about as the unhappy birds shouted their disapproval. I have seen several nests deserted simply because they had been built beside a river and had been passed by harmless fishers intent on their sport. Reading the tracks in the mud, it seemed unlikely that the fishers had visited the nests, but the damage was done, for the cranes, perhaps returning to the nest a time or two, eventually fled in the face of continuing disturbance.

The sandhill as it exists today has good reason for being specific in its nesting requirements. It is a large bird, with a conspicuous, often floating, nest. Such a nest is difficult to hide, except where the marshes are vast in extent or the vegetation heavy, such as on Oregon's Malheur Refuge, in Warner Valley, or the Sycan and Klamath marshes. The bulk of the marshes are small, and the nests easily detected. In response, perhaps, to predation by coyotes, bobcats, and badgers, the cranes, whenever they have a choice, pick a small island of rushes or tall vegetation, completely surrounded by water. If an island is not available, they pick the tip of a narrow peninsula, or, that failing, a wet marsh. During the first stages of rearing chicks the parents keep them in this wet area, then retreat further and further toward dry land as the chick progresses. They are so specialized in their craving that I can survey a marsh and tell where in all that vast sea of vegetation, a crane will decide to nest. I do this quite simply by imagining that I am a Sandhill Crane, and picking the place about me that is the safest from land-roving predators.

Sandhill Cranes, of course, cannot reason in the sense that a human being can. It is instinct in them that compels them to search out a certain type of site. If in time they are compelled to adjust to a different type of environment, they must choose one that will furnish maximum available protection from predation and discovery.

Perhaps their lack of tolerance to continued molestation of the nest results from the fact that bird and nest are conspicuous. A predator can come close to a pheasant's or quail's nest without finding it, since it is not only hidden but without scent, but once an enemy approaches a crane's nest, unless it can be decoyed away or diverted by frantic broken-wing acts on the part of the distraught parents, the nest might just as well be abandoned. When by accident I stumble onto a crane's nest, I simply pass by without stopping or circling the nest, allowing if possible the birds to decoy me away, and they return easily to the nest without delay.

Breeding stimuli, as well as nest safety, are of great importance. So many generations of sandhills, through thousands of years, have been raised under rather specific conditions that perhaps these conditions are necessary for the average sandhill to breed successfully. It is here that imprinting may be a factor.

To explain imprinting, let us be both ridiculous and overly simple. Suppose we have a robin's nest in the bushes in front of the house at Yamsi with four eggs. Two of the eggs are left in the nest to be raised by their parents; the other two eggs are hatched out and raised by hand in our living room. The four young migrate south together and return north the following spring. The pair raised in the bush will go north until some bushes similar to ours cause a breeding response in their glands. The two raised in the living room, in order to have a condition to stimulate breeding, will need, not a bush, but a living room like ours.

What has happened is that in the first hours after hatching the environment has been "imprinted" upon the young birds and has left such an indelible stamp that without this effect of a similar condition the breeding response does not come easily.

There is a practical aspect to all this. A pair of ducks, trapped in the wild as ducklings, may be kept in captivity for years under ideal conditions before breeding, while a pair of ducks, hatched in captivity from wild eggs, will often breed as soon as the ducks reach the normal age for sexual maturity. A similar environment, then, seems necessary for the reproductive cycle to begin.

Resistance to breeding wears off occasionally with time. For no apparent reason, a pair of birds may suddenly reproduce after several unproductive years. When one is attempting to save an endangered species, however, time is of the essence and it is better to begin the building of a captive flock by hatching eggs than by trapping wild birds. Whatever the method used, the establishment of a captive breeding flock is important, for as long as a healthy, captive stock of a species exists, then the continuance of the wild species is far more assured.

The ideal nesting marsh for the Sandhill Crane is in short supply. Nearly every typical nesting area in Oregon able to stimulate a pair of cranes is now occupied. A decade ago there was more than enough marsh to take care of these birds, but this is fast disappearing.

Some of the birds who lost their marsh did not nest again; others moved to lesser, marginal marshes to rear their young. The young of these birds may have been able to change to a less specific type of habitat because they were imprinted with something less than the classic. This gradual adjustment of the species, though slow, enlarges the available habitat by thousands of acres and is one of the heartening things in the battle of the cranes for survival.

But probably this adjustment will come too slowly to be of real help in saving the birds. Left to their own trial-and-error attempts, the cranes will, in all likelihood, attempt nesting in areas where the very conspicuousness of their nests and bodies precludes success. Perhaps through captive management we will be able to imprint young chicks with an environment differing from that of the tule marsh, yet one in which they would have cover—for instance, a considerable expanse of sage such as that which borders many Oregon marshes.

In the Bly Valley, where a rush of land improvement took place around a decade ago, the cranes literally ran out of good nesting sites. In the following years, some failed to nest at all, while one or two homeless pairs adopted less than normal conditions, and I seemed to sense that within a few years conditions had begun to erode somewhat. In an extreme case, one pair nested on dry ground in the Bly Valley in a depression, with no sign of a nest at all. Since the area was so large and removed from habitations, the nesting was actually a success.

Given time, of course, many species could adapt, but conditions now are changing too rapidly for natural adjustment. One drainage ditch, built by a farmer in an afternoon, can lower a water table and ruin a marsh.

The sandhills are highly intelligent birds and respond to protection and good treatment by becoming less wild to their benefactors. The Yamsi cranes are a good example of this. I have poked and prodded my long nose into their business for so long without harming them that they are resigned to my presence and quite tolerant. They have seen me in the company of other cranes, who are obviously anything but afraid. Then, too, a late spring snowstorm often catches them unawares, and in their hunger they soon learn that I am good for a handout. Even the wildest cranes soon come to within a few feet of me, although they are gone the moment a stranger appears.

Animals and birds often have facial expressions that resemble individual humans, making the task of keeping them straight far more simple. One shy little female happens to be "Betsy Palmer," while its tall, somewhat austere mate happens to be "General de Gaulle." I know which female belongs to which male, where they have nested in past years, and how many young they have raised. Fortunately, as I have mentioned, the pairs have the same coloration, the same variation of a basic theme of the natural gray.

The more I work with the cranes, the more I have to come to realize the bewildering complexity of the problems they face. Obviously, it would do no good at all to raise in captivity sandhills that, although completely normal in breeding response, flight abilities, and physique, were tame to humankind. Any birds raised in captivity would merely migrate as had Eeny, Meeny, and Miney, freeloading their way south, unaware of the general dangers of association with an unsympathetic public and causing a sensation wherever they went. I realized clearly that I would have to raise cranes that were truly wild, birds able to fly, able to fend for themselves in the wild, able to accept other sandhills as their own kind, yet wary as far as humans and other predators were concerned.

Furthermore, as far as the work I was doing applied to the even rarer Whooping Crane, opponents of captive management for the Whooping Crane were definitely of the mind that once in captivity the bird would never be more than a sad specimen in a zoo.

Accordingly, we set a single egg under a foster mother experienced in raising baby cranes. We set up opaque panels to form a V, with the open part of the V looking out over natural crane marshes so that the young chick would be properly imprinted with its future habitat. We could approach the pen, however, without being seen by its inhabitants. When, at last, the young crane hatched, we waited until the chick was ready to feed, then, by means of a long tube, dropped meal worms through the wall into a pan of high-protein pheasant crumbles.

The function of the meal worm, a worm common in flour, was twofold, both to serve as an additional source of protein and to add motion to the crumbles. In attempting to stab the worms, the baby got a mouthful of crumbles and eventually began to feed. In time it grew to be a splendid specimen, and from hatching until it was ready to go forth alone did not see a human being.

When the crane became taller than the foster mother and no longer needed her, it drove her off. When the crane became sufficiently large to be safe from Horned Owls, the end of the V panel was slipped away, and the bird was free to wander out among the marshes. While it could supplement its diet from wild sources, it was still free to come back to the pen for food.

I had not reckoned with the fact that the poor crane would not have an association on which to base its identity. Since no other cranes were present, it latched on to the first moving objects taller than it. These happened to be the horses, and the crane assumed he must be one of them.

Seeing this long-legged bird in their midst was too much for my half-broke bunch of cow ponies. For more than an hour they ducked and dodged and galloped themselves into a froth, trying to avoid the bird flying among them. But soon they chose to ignore the affectionate stranger.

Wherever they wandered, the crane marched at their heels, feeding with them on the green meadows, standing in the pines during the heat of the day. As the horses flicked tails against each other's noses, the crane stood preening by, warding off bothering insects by stabbing its beak skyward.

But whenever a cowboy would appear on horseback to run the horses into the corral, the crane would call the alarm and take to the air. The nervous horses would wheel in a circle, looking for danger; then, spotting the wrangler, they would charge off in a high lope, wind in their manes, circling the whole field a dozen times, before finally submitting to the inevitable and galloping on into the corrals.

Before the advent of the crane, we could have walked out and caught any of the older horses with a rope, but now things were changed. From the moment they wheeled off, the crane flew right in the midst of them, spurring them to great bursts of speed, whistling to them excitedly with a plaintive, immature voice. Fleeing like wildfire, they would career away. Invariably, the crane would give a squawk of alarm as the horses burst into the corral and, with wings beating heavily, veer wildly away above the trap. Lonely and puzzled, it would then call nervously from the meadows, until the unused horses were returned to the pasture and it was once again a happy member of the band.

Eventually the bird met others of its species. For a time it seemed torn between the horses and the cranes, but the long absences of the horses as they stood in the corrals finally weaned it away, and, that autumn, in company with wild companions, it migrated to a warmer land.

I spent another one of my long, tense winters staring up at those empty skies. How absolutely sterile they seem when you are waiting for something to fly out of them. And then, one morning, I heard a crane calling out his arrival. A single sandhill cut from a group on high and planed swiftly downward. Right down to its old V panel went the bird and was soon hammering in its feed pan for food.

For some weeks, the young crane hung about the meadows, but when the mature males began to defend their territories in earnest, the young bird felt unwanted, I suppose, for it joined a rootless band of immature cranes, young vagabonds who visited my valley one day and the next were far away.

But what an exciting bird this was to my whole program, indeed to the whole future of the Sandhill and the Whooping Cranes. He was the first captive-raised Sandhill Crane ever put into a wild flock as a fully wild migrating member. With this bird new vistas were suddenly open. No longer were the progeny of captive flocks doomed to being zoo specimens. For the first time, I could do more than dream about taking lonely, craneless valleys and building up a wild population.

Of course there would have to be refinements of techniques. Obviously it would be of advantage to raise a group of cranes at one time, with adjoining V panels, so that, when given their freedom, they would associate with their own kind rather than with a bunch of horses. More than ever now I was convinced that the battle for survival of both the Sandhill and the Whooping Crane could be won by skilled captive management.

CHAPTER

16

Living with Sandy, and with other Sandhill Cranes so much a part of our daily lives, it was easy to forget that beyond our isolated valley the cranes were facing troubled times. A visitor highlighted this for us once when he said, "You don't know how lucky you are with all these Sandhill Cranes. I'm from the Middle West. I loved them as a boy, but I haven't seen one now in over thirty years."

At no time in the history of the universe have wild things been subjected to such swift environmental changes as they face today. The next decades promise to be far more drastic. Left alone, of course, the highly specialized species, such as the California Condor, the Ivory-billed Woodpecker, the Jack-pine Warbler, the Prairie Chicken, the black-footed ferret, the Sandhill and Whooping Cranes, and many others lacking the adaptability or facility for quick adjustment necessary for their survival will soon perish from the earth.

For several reasons, population surveys of the cranes can be highly deceptive. No survey can determine, for instance, the average age of the flock, or the genetic makeup, or the sex ratio,

or the production factor. Failure to adapt will first be evident in a lack of nesting success, where adult birds either make no attempt at nesting, or, upon nesting, fail to rear young. The average age of the existing population increases, of course, with each failure, although the total population decline is at first imperceptibly slow. But tragedy is just a matter of time. Suddenly one year the mean age is old, breeding failures are common, and the species is in swift decline. In the case of the Sandhill and Whooping Cranes, failure to add young adults to the breeding population will mean a swift climb in the average age of the flock. Individual cranes have been known to live thirty to forty years, but these are exceptional birds, and the productive life of the wild bird is far less.

One limiting factor is that the cranes do not breed before their third or fourth year. In the case of the Whooping Crane, whose number is desperately low, production is good, with a fair amount of young birds showing up in the fall at Aransas Refuge, in Texas, for the fall and winter season. But, even if there were a hundred young raised every year and these failed to become breeders, the population would still be headed for disaster when the productive spans of the existing breeders began to run out.

The tragedy is that this is exactly what is happening to limit the crane population. Losses are occurring in the subadults, which means that too few are joining the breeding flock.

Perhaps some insight to this problem of both species comes from looking into the lives of the Sandhill Crane subadults, who during this carefree period of their young lives join together into highly mobile small groups and travel far and wide. As long as the young are with their parents during the winter and spring of the first year, they survive very well. They migrate north with their parents, but on arrival at the breeding grounds, with the subsequent approach of the mating season, they are driven away by the parents to become members of the footloose and fancy-free groups of immatures.

It is at this period when they are forced out into the world by a suddenly vicious parent, left without the comfort and sagacity of mature birds to warn them of dangers, left to shift for a time even without others of their own kind, that they are most vulnerable to loss.

It is important to understand that they are on the breeding ground, or at least well on their way, when this shock comes. The family group might be a hundred miles away from others of the species. The young bird not only must fend for itself but must find other young adults. Usually, when it does locate other cranes, they are breeding pairs and inclined to heap more abuse on it in its already bewildered state. Wandering over the land, there are suddenly new, unfamiliar feeding grounds and dangers, exposure to weather, agricultural poisons, power lines, guns, predators, and all manner of other threats. This, in the case of both the Whooping and Sandhill Cranes, is where the struggle for survival is being lost.

I once assumed that the Yamsi cranes migrated north as a flock, which, upon arrival at the breeding grounds after a joyous journey, broke up into family groups, including the young of

the previous year. In this I erred, for the splitting up into family groups occurs either while still on the wintering ground or on the way north. When the sandhills arrive at Yamsi the families arrive at intervals of a few days and even on arrival are strongly territorial. Their young are tolerated until the approach of the breeding season some weeks later.

In 1965, I witnessed the arrival of each of the Yamsi family groups. By chance, the arrivals were in daylight, and I was off a-horseback on the icy meadows. I heard each first ratcheting goohrah afar in the sterile blueness of the late winter sky.

It so happens that the first weeks of March come at a time when the oppression of winter sours upon a person, and such a harbinger as the arrival of the cranes brings false hope to the summer-loving heart of the oppressed. For it is not really spring when they come each year, yet one expects the back of winter to be broken. Traditionally, however, one is doomed to disappointment; the days seem colder, and the frozen, mildewed grass showing beneath a retreating drift more bleak than ever.

On this particular spring I had been more apprehensive than ever about the arrival of the cranes, for they were two weeks late. Each group announced its arrival in the skies above the east shoulder of Taylor Butte. However much science hates to give birds credit for joys or sorrows, the excitement the cranes exhibited was intense. Like children on the last day of school, they expressed a degree of joy one hears at no other moment of the year. No doubt about their rapture; it is evident to all who listen, and it is not to be confused with any attempt on their part to establish territory, for they have not yet arrived at their territory.

When I finally shielded my eyes with a raised arm to look up into the dazzling sky, the wings of the first pair were already set in a long glide, and they did not flap them again until they reached the ground some three minutes later. Straight to their old domain of the previous year they glided. On landing the male pointed his beak to the skies and announced in no uncertain terms that he was back from the south and henceforth would brook no challenge of his territory by another crane.

Two days later, the second pair sailed over the ridge, along with a young bird of the previous year's hatch. They too, like Eeny, Meeny, and Miney, were excited about coming home and set their wings, clamorous and ecstatic in their joy. Although they too set their gliding course high over the butte it soon became obvious that their glide was taking them farther down the valley to their old territory. Just to make sure, the male who had arrived first at the head of the valley flew up trumpeting loudly, to escort each interloper over the airspace of his domain, and only when the new arrivals had dropped to their old territory, did the male return to his mate.

It is interesting to note that the young crane that came north with this second pair had not yet achieved his mature voice. As he flew over me, he still had the immature piping whistle of a young bird. Other cranes I have known have developed their guttural croakings by early winter, but there seems to be no set rule. The loss of feathers on the crown to form the bare red forehead of the adult is also subject to variation but usually happens to a degree during the first winter.

In like manner, the third family group returned to the valley, and this group glided afar and settled down behind a distant point of pines in what was presumably the Wickiup Springs field.

The young stayed with their parents for from two to three weeks before they were finally driven off. Through past observations, I presume that the male drives off the male offspring, and the female, her daughter, for the males are tolerant of the opposite sex, while the females are quite intolerant of any competition for their mate's affections.

These young are now, of course, deprived of parental wisdom and thus thrown out upon the world very much on their own. Lucky they are if they find an unmated adult to roam with them. The groups are loosely associated, seemingly with little regard for leadership, habit, or tradition. One morning they are here, the next over the neighboring valley's glades, and then far away. They are no longer welcome in this valley of their birth, for this valley is now divided into fiefs, each the property of a savage defending male. The young have no divine right of inheritance. Driven from one fief to another, they must fend for themselves until the following autumn, when the males are sociable once again.

Sandhills are usually strongly territorial, needing in my narrow valley a good country mile between nest sites; but in the open marshes, where the territories extend in all directions from the nest, the nests are much closer together. Here, where there are males on all sides, the territories are harder to defend, and perhaps this makes the male of the wide marshland more tolerant.

However fierce an adversary a crane can be with beak, wing, and toenail, fights are usually vocal but bloodless. Male and female fly at the transgressor, landing beside him. Usually the mere act of walking toward the alien bird is enough to put him to flight and the birds soon establish in this manner just what areas they intend to take as territories. If the cranes were less territorial, far more available nesting areas would open up.

In the case of a species threatened with extinction, however, nature has a distinct task maintaining the genetic health of available blood. The wandering life of the immatures, while causing them great losses, was probably all part of nature's plan, for it did scatter the blood and tend to prevent inbreeding.

If not carefully controlled, inbreeding results in a distinct weakening of the individual bird and low fertility. In the reverse, outbreeding produces vigor and is to be desired. Proper management of a species of low numbers can be best accomplished by intelligent and careful line breeding (mating of related birds), then outcrossing with another successful line. Once numbers are maintained, then enough variation goes on to keep the genetic makeup replenished. In the wild, cranes of a valley tend to line breed; then, when for one reason or another these cranes come into contact with other populations, vigorous matings are the result. Line breeding of cranes is not artificial but nature's way.

One of the best illustrations of the tragedy of inbreeding has been in the Brown-eared Pheasant in captivity. Until recently, all our specimens came from a single trio imported from China years ago. The blood ran out after a bold start. The present Brown-eared Pheasant is a sorry bird indeed, with low vitality, legs often crooked, spraddled, or deformed, and fertility much weakened. Recent new imports of this delightful and personable bird have strengthened the breed dramatically.

Were it not for the fortunate possession of a few good breeding islands in the United States and Canada, the Sandhill Crane might now be in even more extreme danger. In their native, lonely marshes, the sandhills are still able to breed in some number, although by correspondence and by my own flight surveys over nesting grounds, I have never been convinced that there are more than three thousand greater sandhills left. Many of these are too young or too old to breed or for some reason have not found mates.

The fact that there are so many Little Brown, or Lesser, Sandhill Cranes, as well as Canadian intergradients between the greater and lesser, makes an accurate survey difficult. My surveys have been limited to the nesting season, when all breeding cranes in the United States had to be either Greater Sandhill Cranes or the Florida-Mississippi subspecies.

There are two major islands of the greaters, one in Oregon and the other in Michigan, with scatterings in between. Much of the Oregon population exists, not on refuges such as Malheur, but on private land. This is serious, since year by year the cultivation of these privately owned lands is intensifying. Hand in hand with intensive farming comes drainage and loss of breeding marshes to the cranes. This loss will take away Warner Valley, the Chewaucan marshes, the Sycan Marsh, the Bly Valley, Klamath Marsh, Fort Klamath, as well as the valley of the Upper

Williamson. This will leave only a few refuges as breeding grounds for Sandhill Cranes.

Heretofore the cranes have been able to maintain themselves on private land because of the very size of the holdings. The land was bought cheaply in early days, and landowners were able to make a fair return on their investment through somewhat haphazard water use and management, which favored the cranes. Great lonely pieces of land were left in marsh, since quite often development was not economical. Buildings were centralized on the better lands, well away from the breeding and feeding areas.

In the last five years, however, a curious and tragic phenomenon has occurred. Land is being bought up by speculators, who divide the great tracts of land into small acreages and sell them mostly sight unseen to various and sundry sorts, who, in their uprooted existence, feel a basic need to own a few acres of North American land, wherever and whatever they may be. Some of these people are a jobless sort, who, attracted by the small down payments, build shacks upon the land, establish residence, and go on welfare. Land that sold for twenty dollars an acre or less on the basis of its productive powers now often brings eight hundred. With records of such sales in the hands of the tax assessors, a rise in taxes for the legitimate farmer or rancher is inevitable. With higher taxes, more and more ranch and farm land is forced upon the market.

The average income from livestock operations in the West for the past few years has made them marginal investments indeed, so the rise in taxes often throws the already strained budget out of balance. Due to inheritance taxes, the rancher's son has little chance of taking over the family holdings, particularly when the product he sells is based on a 1947 price structure. Ranches seldom if ever go back into local hands; they are bought by speculators for subdividing or by nonresident businesspeople who need a tax advantage for, say, a tool-and-die works in Los Angeles.

These new owners are anything but sentimental about the land. They insist that the lands produce in accordance with the investment, yet very little of the land of southeastern Oregon can even approach earning a fair return. The owner has two choices: to pour in money for the drainage of marshes and intensive development or to sell out through the process of subdivision. In the Bly Valley, eleven of the twelve major home ranches have sold out in the last three years.

By all that is logical, the balloon should have burst long ago, but with our unprecedented prosperity and some land selling in California for as much as forty thousand dollars an acre, there are plenty of Californians who consider land in Oregon a steal, even though they have never been in the state. It matters not if the land is so swampy that a horse couldn't walk across it or so dry a piece of scab-rock desert that there will never be enough soil to support plant life or enough water to make a cup of tea. How I wish I could raise grass as lush or cattle as fat as that person who writes the pamphlets. Yet for the buyers who inspect their purchase and are disillusioned, there is a good chance they can turn right around and find another sucker who will give them more than they gave.

All this is not irrelevant but part and parcel of the destiny of the Sandhill Crane. It is this bird of loneliness that must inevitably lose its marshes to drainage, to the land developer's "cheapie teepie," which is springing weedlike in the midst of former wilderness everywhere.

Everywhere that humans encroach upon the privacy of this great bird the effect is almost certainly a failure to raise young. Not every sandhill hen who is disturbed once on her nest fails to reproduce, but the percentage is there, and there is some evidence that she does not produce well on the year following her disturbance either.

One must bear in mind that during the period of nesting in the West the weather is often unseasonably wintry and the eggs and young susceptible to chill. We are considering a bird that does not nest until it is from three to four years old, a bird that lays only two eggs, and, very often raises only one chick, an immense bird, loud and conspicuous, whose nest is hard to hide, who must live hand in hand with agriculture, and whose chosen home is the fast-disappearing marsh. The Sandhill Crane thrives on loneliness; after the next decade, where shall it go?

CHAPTER

17

Outside of the Little Brown, or Lesser, Sandhill Cranes of the far north, which are here only as winter migrants and in large number, the North American cranes deserve a place on the endangered- species list. Few species of birds in our land today are less understood by the general public.

To summarize the crane situation, there are two species of crane native to North America. One is the Sandhill Crane, which is divided into four subspecies. The greater sandhill is the largest subspecies, represented by Sandy. Greater sandhills exist through the northern states east to Michigan. The lesser sandhill, smallest of the subspecies, nests in the far north. The Florida sandhill nests in the far southeast, and the Cuban sandhill nests in Cuba. There are some forty Sandhill Cranes nesting in Mississippi, small, dark gray birds with roundish heads, which nest in timbered areas and, I feel, may be related to the Cuban sandhill rather than to the Florida. All these subspecies are gray with bare foreheads or crowns of rose caruncles developing usually within the first year.

The only other species of crane in North America is the Whooping Crane, a great white bird with black wing tips and a bare red crown. It is larger than the sandhills and is probably close in relationship to the Manchurian crane of Asia. Sandhill Cranes are far more gregarious than the Whooping Crane, possessing a sociability that ceases abruptly, however, during the breeding season. Even in winter, the Whooping Crane tends to keep in family groups of parents and young of the year.

Historically, the Sandhill Crane was a common resident wherever suitable marshes were found. It suffered to some degree from market hunting before that practice was outlawed, but the greatest factor in its decline has been the drainage of its marsh habitat.

The Whooping Crane was probably always limited, somewhat, to the central flyway. Never very numerous, those cases where it was recorded beyond its range were probably young birds or subadults given to exploring or migrating birds blown off course in storms. Its whooping voice is caused by an elegant set of vocal plumbing, a windpipe, long and convoluted, which far exceeds the sandhill's in length. Its loud voice and conspicuous coloration, both in nesting season and out, and the fact that its range attracted some of the first prairie farmers who drained its nesting marshes and hunted it for food made its life here in any number of exceedingly short duration. Since the late eighteen hundreds, the Whooping Crane has been a rare bird.

In Europe, in the latter part of the eighteenth century, aviculture came into its golden age. Many of the wealthier aviculturists spent huge sums on the importation of exotic species from abroad. Literally hundreds of rare pheasants, such as tragopans, monals, eared pheasants, and firebacks, were imported, some of which existed in captivity until the world wars decimated the captive stock. Such a rare and elegant bird as the Whooping Crane attracted much interest, and collectors were willing to pay a thousand pounds to secure a captive pair. The few birds reaching captivity, however, were destined never to breed and soon died out in collections entirely.

In 1940 there existed two islands of the Whooping Crane, one a resident, nonmigratory colony in Louisiana, the other, a fully migratory population that wintered on the Texas coast and bred at some unknown spot in the far north. Oddly enough these breeding areas remained undiscovered until Robert H. Smith, the famed Fish and Wildlife Service flying biologist, accompanied by Everett Sutton and Bill Cambell, on July 11, 1952, flew over a lone Whooping Crane north of Great Slave Lake. Excited, they returned to the area on July 12, and, forty miles away, spotted a Whooping Crane they thought had chicks. These cranes were in a muskeg, a big, open marsh, scattered with black spruce. These were seen again by seismological crews. The following year the cranes were sighted by a Canadian Forest Service fire team, who returned to the scene with William Fuller, a mammalogist for the Canadian Wildlife Service, who spotted a pair with a young bird near the Sass River. Thus the mystery of the nesting Whooping Cranes was solved.

In 1940, during a tragic cloudburst and flood, the Louisiana flock was blown out of the marshes into farming areas. Those not killed by the violence of the storm were butchered by local residents. The one exception was the famous Josephine, who was taken captive. At Aransas Refuge, Josephine, mated to a large male named Crip, hatched out the first Whooping Crane chick ever hatched in captivity. The cranes were kept in a large marshy compound, however, and the chick disappeared on the fourth day.

Eventually the pair were moved to the Audubon Park Zoo in New Orleans where they hatched out two chicks. *Life* carried a picture story of the triumph, our national guilt at squandering our wildlife heritage was eased, somewhat, and nature lovers, worldwide, rejoiced. I rushed in to town to wire the Audubon Park people that one chick might disappear, but the chick had already vanished, and we never could establish whether or not, like my sandhills, it had been pecked and had run away. The other chick lived for some weeks before it died of aspergillosis. Another milestone, however, had been passed.

In the ensuing years, four young were raised from Crip and Josephine before her death during a hurricane in 1965. Rumor had it that a helicopter, lost during the storm, fighting the winds, had hovered over her building trying to establish its position, and that Josephine died of fright. Whatever the cause, she was gone, and her loss was a great blow to the race, for genetically she was the last remaining member of the resident Louisiana population, as well as the only producing female in captivity. We know that she was at least twenty-six years old and could have been much older.

At one time, at low ebb, the population of Whooping Cranes was fifteen birds. From that low, the flock has made an amazing recovery, swelling to over forty individuals, including six in captivity. In addition to the natural tenacity of the birds themselves, this has been accomplished by a fine educational campaign, international in scope, both up and down the flyway and in the critical wintering area.

But, unfortunately, this does not mean that the future of the Whooping Crane is in any way assured. Various factors could sound the death knell for the race. For one matter, the whole wild flock winters along the coast of Texas at Aransas Refuge, a limited area, and one slightly off-season hurricane could destroy them just as it did the resident Louisiana group in 1940.

Other factors in their destruction might be a sudden toxicity through contamination of the blue crabs and shrimp on which the Whooping Cranes winter; infection of the birds themselves with an avian virus or bacteria; accidental pollution of the area by chemicals from ship or plane; oil-exploration problems; military operations; power lines along the flightways; a small, all-unknowing boy with a twenty-two; poison grain for rodent control along the migration route, which some years ago killed thousands of ducks and geese on the Tule Lake Refuge area in northern California; accumulation of hydrocarbons from insecticides in fatty tissue, resulting in possible death during migration stresses or sterility; molestation of the nesting areas by hunters or prospectors; the building of a railroad or highway in the nesting areas; frequent disturbance in the wintering area by the boating public; vandalism, or even enemy attack; or, most important, the chance introduction of sublethal recessive genes to the genetic makeup of the small population.

In any small, struggling population one risks the chance of damaging genetic introductions. These genetic weaknesses might be present in a perfectly normal-appearing bird and quickly spread through the population. Only when in time recessives mated to each other would the results be damaging. This recessive can be any that lessens the birds' chance of survival, such as a weakness of sperm or embryo viability.

In any captive-management program of the Whooping Crane, records and proper identification of individuals will be imperative. Beef breeds of cattle are only now recovering from the chance introduction of a recessive gene for dwarfism into their bloodlines. Before anyone knew it, this recessive gene had contaminated many of the great herds of the country, but, through records, they were able to isolate the offending beef families and to breed only to those that were genetically clean. The recessive is now but a minor factor.

In the wild, such a factor could have resulted in the demise of many of our now extinct species. The start of any decline in any endangered species should be attacked by establishing genetic islands of blood throughout North America, so that fresh, vigorous blood would be available for outcrossing.

Practically all our Whooping Crane eggs are in one basket, and, until this is changed, the effective end of this great bird could come tomorrow, a grim thought to all those of us who know and love them.

Through the years two contradictory schools have come into being. One school, consisting of the Audubon Society people in the main, thought that the birds should be left to themselves and that time and stringent protection would rebuild their numbers. The other school, consisting of the International Wild Waterfowl Association, as well as some wildlife management people, thought we needed a crash program of research and captive management. My own thought was that, while everything must be done to protect the wild flock and their production, far too much hung in precarious balance to let matters continue in their present state.

I supported this idea on a Whooping Crane panel, which the I.W.W.A. held in Salt Lake City, as well as in a paper read at the Whooping Crane Conservation Association's first convention, in an article in *Audubon Magazine,* and in various other publications.

Both points of view had much to be said for them, and my own feelings might be different if a sufficient number of those birds produced in the wild were going back into the breeding flock. But this is not the case, unfortunately, for the cranes. All too many of the subadult group are vanishing, too few have joined the flock as actual breeders. In any struggle for survival, this factor, and this factor alone, is the determining agent. With every loss of these young potentials, the mean breeding age of the flock goes up, and the population is that much closer to the final abyss.

I favor egg gathering in the wild, because young raised in such a manner are already imprinted with captivity, while it might take years before a wild-caught crane condescends to breed. Josephine, for instance, did not breed for eight years. Capture of Whooping Cranes, too, has had an unfortunate history of hard luck and accidents.

Since few of these Whooping Crane eggs in the wild are actually increasing the breeding flock, losses sustained by the flock would be quite small. Moreover, work with wild sandhills has shown that if the collector straight-lines it past the nest and

picks up one egg without stopping, the hen returns quite readily to the nest and broods the remaining egg.

In the case of the remaining egg, the parents are no longer separated, each with a chick, but both parents stay with the one chick, giving it twice the protection and what amounts to intensified care. The results of intensified care are shown in survival figures of Sandhill Cranes, where the cranes hatch out two chicks yet seldom raise more than one. In a high percentage of cases, however, the pairs do raise that one remaining chick. Whooping Crane twins are also proportionately rare.

What I have long advocated is making every use possible of every Whooping Crane already in captivity. In addition, through cautious implementation by egg gathering from the wild flock, resident or short migratory populations of captive birds could be set up at dispersed points on established refuges throughout the flyway. Here the cranes could be bred and managed on a genetically sound basis to produce as high a number of cranes as quickly as possible. These captive islands should attempt to establish what in livestock genetics would be called a "family."

One such gathering of Whooping Crane eggs has now taken place. Dr. Ray Ericson flew the eggs from the north to the new crane refuge in Patuxent, Maryland. Of six eggs, five were hatched and are doing well. Follow-up reports from biologists in the north indicate that the Whooping Cranes hatched out the one egg left in each nest (one egg taken, one egg left).

Genetically speaking, the fact that there were two islands of population so far separated as Louisiana and Wood Buffalo Park was of great importance, for effective line breeding, much as that which I proposed, was actually taking place. With every generation, some genetic variation was going on.

The outcrossing of these two lines with the mating of Josephine from the southern, nonmigratory group and Crip from the northern group may have accounted for some of their success and the fertility of her eggs. This Louisiana blood could be quickly lost by diffusion into the common pool, unless the offspring of this mating are kept carefully separate or used to establish a third island. In other words, line breeding must be practiced in selection of mates, so that the genetic material Josephine carried can be kept alive.

There is also the grave danger that Josephine and her Louisiana group were losers, a genetic group of low vitality or possibly with harmful recessives bred into them. We must remember that even without the storm of 1940, this population was having a difficult time. Possibly the whole flock had been started many years ago by a few cripples, and inbreeding had deteriorated the stock; perhaps they no longer possessed genes for migration, so that their offspring would never be able to function as a migratory flock. Until the capabilities of this stock for survival in the wild are proven, it should be kept separate from the northern stock.

Once the value of this blood could be proven by establishment of a third colony of northern-southern blood, it might, of course, be found that the end product was a bird stronger and more productive than either group.

I am not saying it will be simple. One simply does not put two mature cranes together and say, "Now lay some eggs." The way will be hard, filled with frustration, and will take popular and congressional support, but it seems the best way to effect their survival.

One of the major arguments of the group against captive management is that we will end up with nothing but a bunch of zoo birds, and certainly, had I stopped experimenting with Sandy, Eeny, Meeny, Miney, and Moe, I should have tended to agree. It seemed for a long time that the very dependent nature of the bird was to preclude any possible success.

However, the Great Auks, the Dodos, the Heath Hens, the Passenger Pigeons, and the Carolina Parakeets gathering dust in various museum collections are a long way from the regeneration of their species, and every year aviculture makes some heartening breakthroughs with difficult species.

I feel that success at Yamsi in raising Sandhill Cranes in captivity and flighting them as fully wild birds capable of migration and return to home base the following spring is an important step. What can be done with the sandhills should be possible with the Whooping Cranes. Aviculturists who have worked successfully with most of the diverse families of cranes in the world, from the dainty demoiselle to the giant saurus, claim no important difference in them.

To most dedicated conservationists, the word "captivity" is anathema. Somehow it conjures up a canary-in-the-cage picture in the heart of the lover of nature. Fortunately, crane management does not require more than large protected areas for the management of breeders. Young, of course, must be protected from predation, but large fenced areas of marshes with an abundance of natural food are possible when predation is rigidly controlled. I have recently been able to manage full-winged adults with no fence at all, using the territoriality of the males to form invisible divisions.

Twenty years ago, the feeding of the more sensitive species in captivity was a difficult thing. Now modern science has come up with feeds, medically supplemented, vitamin enriched, high in available protein, with which one can grow a perfect specimen of everything from a hummingbird to a condor.

The present wild population of Whooping Cranes has a difficult problem in that its nesting ground is so far north. While on one hand it is protected by loneliness, on the other hand the shortness of the nesting season makes unlikely the possibility of a second clutch if the first clutch is destroyed. At Yamsi, by gathering eggs from two different nestings, one captive, one wild, we forced a production of eight young birds, where four would have been optimum under natural conditions and two would have been average, since most wild cranes raise but one to a pair. In each case, captive and wild, the second clutches were able to migrate by fall. In the north, of course, any cranes unable to migrate by fall for any reason soon perish from lack of food.

Islands of Whooping Cranes established in warmer climes would not have this factor to contend with. They would have not only a longer nesting and renesting season but a shorter migration route, less subject to the dangers of stopovers, and they would arrive in the breeding area in stronger condition.

On the negative side would be the fact that young of the year would have to spend their first year closer to the hazards of civilization, but perhaps good educational campaigns could help lessen this hazard.

Every year I seem to stumble upon things that make the management of cranes easier. The devotion of a Sandhill Crane to its mate, for instance, is a stronger force than migration. Where one of a pair is crippled, the full-winged mate will remain as long as food is available.

This loyalty of a mate could be of considerable help in establishing colonies of breeding cranes. It also could explain how such a colony as the resident Louisiana population might have evolved naturally in the first place. While all islands of cranes nesting between Louisiana and Wood Buffalo Park could have died out, leaving two extremes of population, it now seems to me more likely that the colony arose from cripples, whose mates stayed loyally by them on the wintering ground, until, eventually, a breeding colony was formed. This was probably an inbred group, which may have contributed to their lack of success.

Certain problems of winter food and range exist for the Whooping Crane. Since they are territorial even in winter and favor more animal protein in their diet, they need far more specific a wintering area than the grain-loving sandhills. The tidal marshes they seem to favor are limited and are subject to pressures of increasing land use and oil development. But research in feeding other specialized birds and animals has indicated that some "tastes" can be changed. It would seem worthwhile to attempt to interest the Whooping Cranes in other types of winter food, thus enlarging the potential winter area, but this must be carefully thought out, since supplemental feed such as sweet potatoes or grain might merely attract other species, like lesser sandhills, to a point above the population tolerance of the Whooping Cranes. Then, too, developing a taste for agricultural food might cause the cranes to wander farther afield and stray too far from the comparative safety of the refuge, making them unpopular with the natives. A crop such as acorns might be of more value. Winter-food research will play a huge part in a determination of the future of the Whooping Crane.

CHAPTER

18

Seventeen years ago, when I first began to work actively with Sandhill Cranes, I did so because no one else seemed worried enough to undertake such work. The Fish and Wildlife Service officials, while sympathetic, were unconcerned. Since the cranes were not a hunted species, they felt that public money should not be used to research cranes, however endangered they might be. While Lawrence Walkinshaw, a dentist from Battle Creek, Michigan, had published an excellent, scholarly study of the Sandhill Cranes, his work did not attempt to enter the areas in which I was most concerned, those of management and the salvation of the species. Of both the Whooping Crane and the Sandhill Crane, much was as yet unknown

For instance, no one knew the exact period of incubation; there was no method of sexing cranes cloacally; captive management and breeding techniques were almost unknown; even simple matters of chronological development, such as when the brown eye of the chick becomes yellow, when the voice matures, when the crown becomes bare, when the bird reaches sexual maturity, were guesswork. Yet all these questions had a bearing on determining age of existing populations or on management practices. The most burning question of all was whether or not the Sandhill and Whooping Crane could be put back into nature as wild birds, if someone were lucky enough to breed them. Then, too, what sort of production might one expect from captivity? If production did not exceed that of which the wild birds were capable, it would hardly be worthwhile to propagate them.

However large these birds were, they were birds of loneliness and difficult to observe. Even today, artists who draw the Whooping Crane, for instance, persist in placing the tertial plumes of the wing on the tail. When the bird is at rest these wing plumes do seem to be tail feathers, but when the wing is raised for flight, or in the dance, these feathers, which curve outward from the body, are no longer covering the tail but are flight feathers. The tails of all the species of cranes that I have seen are straight feathered, much on the order of that of the Canada Goose.

Photo by Jon Brenneis

Even today there is a misconception amongst some wildlife people, perhaps through confusion with herons, that the cranes eat fish. Recently, I was a guest speaker at an Izaak Walton Club meeting in Portland, Oregon, and to my horror I was introduced to those august fishers as an expert on Sandhill Cranes and other "fish-eating" birds. I explained as unemotionally as I could that fish were not really part of their diet.

Only when captive Whooping Cranes were put under twenty-four-hour surveillance was it discovered that the whoopers copulate standing up and, usually, in the morning. Last year I was able to confirm that wild sandhills also copulate in this manner. I had been watching this performance for years and had been so conditioned with the supposition that they squatted like a barnyard hen that I had not realized what I was seeing. The sandhills I watched, however, mated at 7:10 one evening, as a climax to a courtship dance.

Sandhills do squat but I have always maintained that this has nothing to do with sex and is more a greeting ritual done by male and female alike. Observation of copulation, of course, strengthens my theory, for there is no similarity between the two actions.

At the time I applied for my first permits to hold Sandhill Cranes for research purposes, I had no idea that the relationship between the Fish and Wildlife Service and private aviculture was severely strained, due to some undue suspicion on both sides. Besides the Sandhill Cranes, I was concerned with duck and goose nests doomed for one reason or another to destruction. It seemed that these eggs could be hatched out by an interested individual such as myself and released to the wild. Upon application, I was immediately suspected of wanting to eat those I raised or to sell them to other individuals for lots and lots of money.

Suddenly, a Fish and Wildlife enforcement officer, sent to investigate me, appeared and spent the better part of a week sitting in his automobile atop the hill overlooking the Bly Valley, watching me through his binoculars. Whenever I arrived in the morning, he was sitting there, and he remained until I left at night.

It was great fun being watched. Often when we would catch the flash of binoculars in the sunlight, we would go through all manner of suspicious actions. I finally took to sitting with him in his car, which so exasperated him that he began doing his research on me in the town of Bly and spent so much time interrogating my poor wife and frightening the baby with his gruff, unsmiling ways that Gerdi locked the door on him.

I complicated matters by lending him and his assistant a couple of gentle horses to make a goose-brood count the valley, and they managed to traverse most of the marshland before being bucked off and stranded miles from their car.

Somehow, the permit came through in spite of all this. In the years since, Yamsi has been a way station for many of Fish and Wildlife Service's dedicated employees, who came forewarned that they would have to spend hours listening to me discourse on my beloved cranes. The association has been for me, through the years, one of exceeding richness. The aura of suspicion that once shrouded the relationship of aviculture with the Service has long since been dispelled by a liaison between the two and the mutual respect one dedicated group has for the other.

Perhaps I have carried the matter of a captive audience a little too far, but it has all been for the welfare of the cranes. Once I watched in horror as a government helicopter landed in one of my crane marshes. Lurking in the brush on my horse, I waited until the occupants had waded through an awful bog, then spurred on out over the meadow and threatened to gutshoot the helicraft. I managed to capture the lot of them as they ran through the bog, then kept them standing in the mud for a half-hour while I lectured them on the irreparable damage they had done my nesting sandhills. By the time I had finished, the men were so interested in Sandhill Cranes that they invited me to go with them on their flights over Oregon's marshlands. While they did their work, I was able to make my first real survey of populations and nesting success.

So much did I learn in this survey that I began to haunt Fish and Wildlife pilot Bob Smith to take me along on his waterfowl-survey flights over the crane areas of eastern Oregon. For several years, Bob has flown from the far north to Mexico making the waterfowl counts that help determine the annual migratory-waterfowl bag limits. Since he seldom flies his big twin-engine amphibian more than three hundred feet above

the ground, flying with him calls for a strong stomach on the part of the passenger. It seemed but one more thing I could do for Sandy and the cranes. All would have gone well had not Tom Garratt, now head of enforcement for the region, called me to tell me that the only way to fly with Bob was to sit down and eat five pounds of ripe bananas.

Bob's big mistake was to ask me to ride in the cockpit with him. We had just landed in Lakeview, Oregon, after a very sick flight, when the bag the pilot had so thoughtfully provided for my illness blew up with the pressure difference and splattered all over the pilot and the interior of the cockpit. This was, perhaps, the low ebb of relationships between the Service and aviculture, and I've heard it rumored that the reason the Service eventually disposed of the plane was that it was easier to sell the plane than to clean it.

Those flights over Oregon's major crane areas, however, did convince me that in this stronghold of the Greater Sandhill Crane there were not so many cranes as had been supposed.

This lent new impetus to my work and made me try even harder to convince the Fish and Wildlife Service that they should begin a real crash program of researching the cranes while there was time to save them.

When I was again advised that there was no money to carry out this type of study, even though it would surely be of concern to both the future of the Sandhills and the Whooping Cranes, I plunged back into my own research on the problems. Sandy and the group she had started seemed more important than ever.Through the ensuing years we blundered along slowly, making what progress we could, publishing our findings and theories in various magazines, writing letters, and buttonholing whoever would listen.

Several pressures were building on the Fish and Wildlife Service through the years, compelling them to action. The Audubon Society people, as I have said, were pushing protection as the solution for Whooping Crane survival, and the International Wild Waterfowl Association, of which I was a director, favored the captive- management program. The Service was caught directly in the middle.

Then, too, the flocks of little brown, or lesser, sandhills were causing damage to crops in parts of the Southwest where they congregated in huge flocks, and the Service was put under pressure for an open season on these birds so that the hunters could harvest the obvious surplus. Since little was known of the wintering habits of the greater sandhill, I was concerned lest this endangered bird be mistakenly shot as a lesser.

And there was the great chance that the lesser bird's unpopularity would slop over and hurt its endangered and embattled cousins, the Greater Sandhill and the Whooping Crane, once crane hunting was given publicity as a new and exciting sport by the hunting magazines, who, as I have said, were wont to lump all the subspecies together.

In order to calm the fears of those of us who thought that rare cranes might suffer by this open hunting season on the lesser, the Service, at last, began a study of cranes.

It is really a sad commentary on our times that we are interested in birds just in terms of killing them or in terms of how much powder and shot are expended, how many sporting goods are sold. American commercialism has had a great stake in determining which birds were called valuable or rated a research program. For too many years the defenders of the nonsporting birds have been individuals such as myself or such selfless organizations as the National Audubon Society, whose tireless work has saved many species from extinction.

Perhaps, also, the government has realized that there is a larger force than the hunter in full cry across the land, and that is the recreationist, who gets a real thrill out of just seeing wildlife and who has a real desire to see an end to tragedy.

At any rate, the Fish and Wildlife Service has come up with a program of research for endangered species, which will concern itself, among other things, with the problem of cranes. The Service first sent Tom Burleigh, an ornithologist with the University of Idaho, to visit Yamsi, and then biologist Irv Boeker.

Of immediate concern was the problem of cloacal sexing of cranes, and all I accomplished along this line was to get a lot of cranes mad at me and to determine that some sort of instrument would have to be devised for the job.

Begun in Monte Vista, Colorado, with Sandhill Cranes, the Service's program has now been moved to Patuxent, Maryland, and, thanks to the dedication and foresight of Senator Karl Mundt of South Dakota who had the courage to sponsor the required legislation, the program promises real hope for vanishing species.

This research was put in the hands of some knowledgeable and dedicated people, such as Eugene Dustman, Director of Patuxent, Assistant Director Ray Ericson, and Chief of the Department of Propagation at Patuxent Gene Knoder. Both Ray Ericson and Gene Knoder have spent time with me at Yamsi and are careful men who will work hard and selflessly to save endangered species.

But, however wise and dedicated the personnel chosen for this work, there is one small fear I cannot hide. Too often in government, priorities arise that involve the transfer of key personnel to other projects. Death of key people might be only as far away as a plane crash, a heart attack, or a freeway accident. In such a case, new personnel would have to take over, and a study of the reports of one's predecessor is no substitute for experience. Avicultural battles are won by attention to tiny details; the disregard of any one can result in total failure.

For this reason, I think it vital that a competent board of biologists and aviculturists frequently review at Patuxent each tiny detail of the project. In the past, mistakes with the Whooping Crane have been made that would never have happened had such a board been in close attendance.* This board, of nongovernment people, with no careers at stake, could speak boldly and could add continuity during the inevitable changes of personnel.

Certainly crane research will unearth no instant solution to assure the birds a place of permanence on this green earth. The way for these huge birds will always be difficult, and the end of our cranes will be forestalled only as long as there are those of us who care and are willing to work hard and long to make an accomplished fact of their continuing survival. Crane research cannot work miracles; the real destiny of the crane lies in the hands of the people and in their willingness to support programs to ease its way. Like the rumble of wagon wheels, the sound of Whooping Crane and sandhill alike is part and parcel of the history of our land and our western heritage. The battle cry of the Comanche is gone, and the thunder of vast herds of bison, but the sound of the crane still rolls faint and far across the prairies. We cannot let it die, for once silent all the science in the world cannot bring it back.

To watch those great wings circling high over Yamsi and my valley, and to know in my heart that without me some of them would not be there, that is my satisfaction. It will be a sad and empty spring when I can no longer look up into an awakening sky and shout for all to hear, "The cranes are coming!"

---

*I advised that bantams be used on the Whooping Crane eggs at New Orleans instead of artificial incubation. Japanese silkies, noted for close setting, were used, and some eggs were ruined because no one thought to cool the eggs. A gentle feather-type bantam would have been better, and the eggs should have been cooled and kept moist. Capable aviculturists would have picked up this detail immediately.

CHAPTER

19

Whatever success is eventually achieved in raising the cranes in captivity, their whole future is tied up in the willingness of the agricultural community to make a real effort to help them. The same is true of course for most wildlife species alive today. Their salvation depends upon an agricultural future; but problems do exist that seriously becloud what is in store for them.

Just like wildlife, the agricultural industry faces a complexity of problems, and in many areas a real fight for survival. In the cattle industry the old cattle barons are things of the past; they have been replaced by young, often college-educated moderates, who are of a new climate, a new responsibility, engendered by the realization that times are changing and that they face, along with the rest of the world, tremendous and serious problems.

Agriculture faces, on the one hand, the staggering task of raising enough food and fiber for a burgeoning population, two-thirds of which, on a world basis, goes to bed hungry and, on the other hand, the problem of furnishing more and more recreation and wildlife use of these private lands. By 1970, United

States population is expected to reach 214 million and, by 2000, a projected 380 million.

Consider the rapid change that has taken place in the past five years. Hunters once had tremendous political power, but now they are suddenly becoming a minority. Less and less land is available for hunting; bag limits are so restricted as to be economically hardly worth the effort. Movement of the rural population to the city, coupled with a deification of the idea that the country is the only place to raise children and that a week spent out there with the kids in the woods will somehow eradicate what fifty-one weeks of neglect have produced, has helped make outdoor recreation a national hysteria. This is the coming era not of the hunter but of the recreationist, a city-oriented body who will wield tremendous power in Congress and will determine the whole future relationship of agriculture and recreation in the United States.

Right now, 40 percent of our population was not around when the bomb dropped. By 1970, there will be 100 million Americans twenty-five and under. They will be more interested in rockets than sporting guns, and we who love to crouch at dawn in the cold misery of a duck blind or hunt quail over a brace of setters will be vastly outnumbered by those who are content just to see a flock of Canada Geese land in a stubble field.

I am a hunter, too, but slowly the hunting has become more important than the shooting. Watching my setters work, the near stroke I have when a rooster ringneck explodes beneath my feet, these are the things I value. I find a certain relief, suddenly, in a shot missed, a certain sense of guilt in the marred beauty of a dog-mouthed bird. I was raised in the hunting tradition, but even in me something has begun to happen; there is a voice warning of coming scarcities, there is apprehension for the future; there is a fear of the unknown quality of the voices of majorities soon to govern the land.

How far away really is the day when we go hunting on opening day without guns, with a pair of binoculars by Winchester, with a special new wildlife camera by Remington Arms, with ultrafast color film by DuPont Powder? We'll come home excited by trophies, but we'll need Eastman Kodak, not a taxidermist, to prepare them for our study walls.

Population control could avoid all this, of course, but by the time we become so crowded as to be uncomfortable and frightened enough to act, we shall long ago have lost our wildlife heritage.

In the past we could look to the great reservoir of public lands, but in the last few years land pressures have shot up, forcing wildlife more and more to the use of private lands. Much of the public domain is the land nobody wanted, and much of this is unfit for wildlife, since there is little food. Eighty percent of the United States is private land. Three-quarters of the small-game and bird harvest in the United States is on private land. Eighty percent of the total feed and forage for all game and wildlife comes from private land. Of this private land, it is chiefly agricultural land that bears the large burden of supporting wildlife.

When my uncle came to the Klamath Basin in 1906, there were few deer in spite of a good summer supply of forage. Lack of food during periodic hard winters limited the deer population, and predators were common. With agricultural development of the area, deer populations were no longer forced to starve in the winter, and the numbers boomed. On my own ranch I have counted one hundred seventy-four mule deer in one herd. We are surrounded by excellent deer ranges, but the supplementary needs of these deer are so great that we are unable to grow conventional high-production crops such as alfalfa or clover.

Many people think a refuge system would be the answer for our wildlife, but the refuge people themselves realize that the new pressures of land use have pretty much limited their expansion and that it is increasingly difficult to procure funds for the development of existing lands.

I myself believe that private agricultural land holds the answer to the future of wildlife. Yet the farmers and ranchers are not being asked to help but are being fought on all fronts by a general public who should be out knocking on front gates asking for aid.

Vast areas are being sterilized now for wildlife use, because ranchers or farmes are bewildered by the tremendous population pressures outside their fences and cannot cope with them. It is far easier to drain their marshes, because marshes raise wildlife, and wildlife attracts people, and people cause trouble, and trouble they have enough of already.

Their investment of many years of hard labor lies not in the bank where it can be guarded, but spread over the land as crops, livestock, machinery, or land improvements. These things are vulnerable to theft or vandalism. Who pays when one gate is left open and the bulls get in with the heifer calves and they die calving too young? Who pays when the cows get into the alfalfa and die of bloat, although in each case the damage might amount to thousands of dollars? What protects ranchers from a lawsuit for damages from a hunter-caused fire that has spread from their property to damage that of a neighbor?

One law alone protects them from invasion, and that is the trespass law, a misdemeanor law at best. They live in a lonely land, without police protection, vulnerable to city hoods and vandals. They are the garbage dump, the outdoor toilet of the encroaching city.

In the West, on public ranges, ranchers have been spending thousands of dollars of their own money, working with their own labor and equipment, to build up the arid land. They are working side by side with Forest Service Bureau of Land Management and university technicians to raise forage where none grew, to develop water where none was, and to increase the natural resources, without which there is no new wealth. They are the ones living adjacent to these public lands and the ones most concerned if disaster strikes.

The great urban population murmurs, "Kick the cattle off the western lands, and we'll have a great big deer park." They do not realize that our summer ranges are generally ample for both wildlife and livestock use and can be developed tremendously in the full framework of the multiple-use theory. For much of the year, during critical winter months, wildlife shares the private lands with the cattle. If all the cattle were driven from the western ranges, wildlife would still have to winter on private lands.

One would think that farmers, faced with the frustrations caused by the public, would protest angrily, but they chew placidly enough on their timothy stalk and go on being a friend to wildlife. And herein lies the glimmering of hope for cranes and other endangered species.

A rancher in South Dakota is working with Fish and Wildlife Service biologists to set aside some of his land for prairie-dog colonies, to save the black-footed ferret from extinction. In Florida, the Audubon Society has enlisted the aid of ranchers and wangled leases for over half a million acres of ranch land held to be critical for the survival of the Bald Eagle—land money could not have bought. A rancher in Texas has booted his cattle off a sizable area of his own land to make room for endangered African species. In my own case, 25 percent of my arable land is maintained in marshes as a nesting place for cranes and other species. Great Gray Owls and eagles nest unmolested in my forests.

Most of the people in agriculture are naturalists at heart or they wouldn't put up with the scant 2 percent they get on their investments. They would like to help wildlife, but they want to be asked, they want to be understood and appreciated, and above all, they want to be protected by law from human depredation before they can unrestrainedly invite wildlife and the public upon their private lands.

Up to now, we have pretty much enjoyed hunting and fishing to the best standard our underfinanced game commissions could provide. There is hope that the farmers will someday throw the full power of their ingenuity and energy into producing a degree of wildlife management and recreation as a crop that will be superior to our wildest dreams. There is hope that citizens will take upon themselves some of the responsibilities of law enforcement by making citizen's arrests of those they find disobeying any of the many laws that concern human behavior in rural areas.

More and more of our population will be made up of young people; there is no better time than now to take children into the country, even if it must be through the educational medium of films, to teach them their responsibilities as good citizens, pointing out to them that much of the future of wildlife is dependent upon their good behavior and their ability to bring into the fold for wildlife the vast reservoir of private lands.

Actually, a senseless war goes on, not between nations, but between agriculture and the public, a war neither can win but both must lose. The tragedy is that when elephants fight it is the ant who is trampled; in this case, the ant is our vanishing wildlife heritage. Eighty percent of our wildlife is dependent, not upon the government, but upon private agriculture for its livelihood; the fate of many species, such as the Sandhill Crane, lies in the hollow of the farmer's hand. Yet no legislation could possibly force farmers to shoulder the burden of wildlife; no legislation could force them to care. If, in the end, they come to care, it will have to be because they want to care.

If the public is at fault for not understanding the problems of agriculture and, indeed, aggravates the fight, the farmers and ranchers have really done little to state their case. Yet how thoroughly the welfare of each group is entwined with that of the other. Pick up any magazine, read how villain farmers created the dust bowl, how they are destroying wildlife with pesticides, how they are draining the marshes. School movies show them plowing up duck and pheasant nests, clearing the forests for crops, taking water from the rivers, fencing off their land from public access, costing the public money by growing too much grain.

Every such attack widens the rift, drives away the greatest potential ally wildlife ever had. Good farming is, in most cases, bad wildlife management. Farmers drain their marshes, not only to farm more intensely, but because the marsh attracts hunters who leave their gates open and shoot their livestock. They plow up their hedgerows, not only to halt the spread of noxious weeds, but to cut down on the number of pheasants and quail, which, in turn, attracts fewer hunters to trample their crops. Even if there were no hunters, the feed required to support wildlife on any farm or ranch amounts to a measurable percentage of the income.

It would be far better for the public to say, "Farmer, we need your help. Much of our remaining wildlife looks to your private land for food to eat, a home, a nesting place, a place to rest. Please create a small marsh, a pond, a woodland, a brush patch, or a fence row on your place; please spare some winter food for wildlife when they are faced with starvation. We appreciate the fact that this will take sacrifice and effort on your part, money out of your pocket, and for this we will thank you by trying to understand your problems, by teaching our children by example to keep your fields free of garbage, to close gates and be careful with fire and firearms, to avoid vandalism. We shall teach them that the country is your home and we are but guests therein."

All over the land, given this new appreciation, farmers will cooperate with the public, for they were naturalists before the public was, and a love of wildlife is inherent in their very nature. If the public will work with farmers and not against them, they will accept the challenge, create a small marsh here, a haven there, which, nationwide, will add up to an effective refuge no government in the world could match.

CHAPTER

20

Sandy is gone now, buried beneath the base of the giant ponderosa pine that stands, oddly cranelike and alert, overlooking the ranch house, the family, and the valley that she loved. Already her body, entwined with roots, has become a part of the sturdy vigor of the tree itself, giving her centuries more of life. The winds, fingering the branches of the landmark pine, murmur, softly, a song to her and sound like the whispering caress of crane wings from somewhere in an evening sky. Her name, carved in the bark, has already begun to weather with the winter storms and is yellow with the golden amber of encrusted pitch. She is gone, but in no sense is she forgotten.

It is safe now for women to wear slacks; Gerdi's laundry comes in clean from the line; there is no longer one who stands constant vigil over us as we sleep. No more is the front porch covered with piles of night-shredded moth wings, and the croak of joy she used to give me when she saw me is stilled forever. Jet aircraft violate our airspace at will, without being challenged. Chances are our youngest children, John and Taylor, will never amount to much, for they will have to grow up without her

nurse-maiding ways. For almost sixteen years, Sandy dominated my marriage like a termagant mother-in-law, and now that she is no longer there to edge between us as we walk, Gerdi and I hardly know what to do with our new-found freedom.

From the moment of her chaotic emergence from a storm-tossed egg in an incubator at Bly, she seemed destined for survival in spite of all. Surely, this vain, difficult, often pathetic bird was singular in the unique gift she gave her fellow creatures. Sandy breathed the element of hope, for the first time, into the whole new concept of aid for endangered species. What followed at Yamsi, through the years, would not have come about had not she paved the way, set up the whole incredible series of events that are now avicultural history and have so considerably brightened the future of the Sandhill Crane and the Whooping Crane alike. Because of Sandy, and because through her we were able for the first time in history to put cranes raised in captivity back into the wild as fully wild, migrating, producing birds, there is new hope that people, fired by a new sense of responsibility, can help a species threatened with extinction adjust to the tremendous pressures of our changing times.

Because of her we were able to discover the production capabilities of captive management, as opposed to the wild.

Sandy may have been of great importance not only to rare and endangered species but to all wildlife, for she initiated an awareness in the minds of ranchers such as myself that private agricultural land could and should function as a great refuge for American wildlife. This germ of an idea, which has found such wide acceptance, properly nurtured, blessed with help and understanding from the public, stands fair to become one of the most vital and dramatically helpful wildlife-management ideas of the times.

Her wings were still, I noticed, as she glided over the marshes on her evening flight, but there was the joy of youth in her voice as she sailed high above the surrounding ridges and hurled her stentorian challenge at the world beneath her. Some premonition, perhaps, made me watch her as she sailed high, cleaving the warm, sweet summer air with her giant wings.

Spreading my fingers out like pinion feathers, I flapped my arms awkwardly, bouncing clumsily over the meadow as I ran, and she called down to me, laughing hoarsely at our private joke.

"The old man's trying to fly again," Dayton said to his sister, Ginny, while Marsha giggled, and John and Taylor looked interested as though they expected me to become airborne any moment. My wife breathed an audible sigh, but I'm sure all of them knew, somehow, what was in my heart.

She flew over joyfully, reviewing us as troops all out for inspection. We could hardly remember life without her, and as she swept high we were looking at a decade and a half of Yamsi history.

When Sandy returned from her evening tour, a cool wind was already settling in my valley's glades. She seemed visibly tired as she settled into her long glide, and, suddenly, I saw that her speed was carrying her past the meadows toward the corrals. She tried desperately to brake as she soared over, just missing the tops of the pines.

Near the barn is a small, round horse corral of heavy logs, high-walled for breaking horses. Frantically, Sandy tried to land in the corral, but the angle was too great and she crashed into the heavy wall of logs.

She lay quietly in my arms as I carried her toward the house. Her hip was broken, one long leg hung useless, pendulum-like, and there was no hope for her. Some distance from the stream, the old crane struggled to get down, and I laid her on a bed of clover, surrounded by a profusion of blue penstemon, meadow gentian, blue-eyed grass, and Indian paintbrush. For a time, I sat with her on the bank, talking softly, as if I could by my clumsy, inadequate words help somewhat to ease the pain. She blinked her great yellow eyes as though mystified at the swiftness of it all, and I left her then to cross the log bridge and call Gerdi and the children. She watched me go, her head erect, beak slightly parted, long legs folded beneath her, still proud, still full of her love for me. It was my last glimpse of her alive.

When we came back, some moments later, Sandy, like some gray, feathered Ophelia, had gone down to the stream and drowned herself in the placid water and was but a ruffled gray island, floating gently toward the home of the north winds, down the quiet currents of the Yamsi brook.